PIONEERING ORGANIZATIONS

the convergence of

Individualism

Teamwork

and

Leadership

LARRY N. DAVIS

Executive
Excellence
Publishing

For permissions requests, contact the publisher at:
    Executive Excellence Publishing
    1344 East 1120 South
    Provo, UT 84606
    phone: 1-801-375-4060
    toll free: 1-800-304-9782
    fax: 1-801-377-5960
    email: info@eep.com; web: www.eep.com

For Executive Excellence books, magazines and other products, contact Executive Excellence directly. Call 1-800-304-9782, fax 1-801-377-5960, or visit our Web site at www.eep.com.

Printed in the United States

10 9 8 7 6 5 4 3 2 1

Cover art by Warren Cullar
Cover design by Jim Easley
Interior graphics by Terry Johnston of NGN Worx

Printed by Publishers Press

Library of Congress Cataloging-in-Publication Data

Davis, Larry N., 1941-
  Pioneering organizations : the convergence of individualism,teamwork, and leadership / Larry N. Davis.
    p. cm.
Includes bibliographical references (p. 262) and index.
  ISBN 1-890009-84-9 (hard : alk. paper)
  1. Organizational effectiveness. 2. Organizational change--United States.
3. Individualism--United States. 4. Teams in the workplace--United States.
5. Leadership. I. Title.
  HD58.9 .D38 2000
  658.4'092--dc21
                        00-008278

To my father

Walter Woodrow Davis
1919–1995

whose legacy was the gift of pioneering vision

"Larry has a knack for seeing the critical issues, facing them, and making sure that performance improves in the process. With the rapid change we face, his approach has been critical."

—J. Merritt Belisle
CEO, Classic Communications

"Larry Davis focuses on ordinary organizations doing extraordinary things. He captures the essence of the why and how of innovation in today's world."

—Dr. Robert Ronstadt
Director, IC² Institute

"To be included in this dynamic book is truly inspiring. The challenge of being in front is always interesting, tenuous, and rewarding. *Pioneering Organizations* will be my guide."

—Larry Callahan
Ranch Manager, Post Ranch Inn

"*Pioneering Organizations* is about the forces behind fiscal responsibility, about open meetings, about sending signals to teams, and about getting everyone's interests converging to unleash high levels of productivity. Larry Davis is onto something here. This book provides the whys and many of the hows of pioneering. It will change the way you think about management techniques, organizational structures, and team dynamics. It will help you think like an industry pioneer."

—Neil Webber
Co-founder, Vignette Corporation

Acknowledgments

*T*his book is dedicated, first and foremost, to my magnificent seven. These are six of the most outrageous individualists I've ever known, and a seventh who may outdo us all:

To *Chip Bell*, a true friend who badgered, called forth, encouraged, praised, crossed out, and suggested this book into being. Chip also first suggested the word *pioneering* to capture what I was trying to describe.

To *Patricia Otis Stephens*, who has given me my most endearing and enduring friendship, who has always raised my vision, tested my beliefs, challenged my nonsense while praising my good sense when it appeared, and who envisioned the right path for this book.

To *Maxine Bozeman Davis*, who, along with my father when he was living, taught me the importance of forming my own beliefs, fighting for them when needed, and being willing to strike out into the unknown to find a better path for us all. These gifts formed the basis for pioneering vision.

To **Zach**, **Andrea**, and **Savannah Davis**, who gave me home, family, and inspiration for the beginning of the journey and who constantly let me see what extraordinary, loving people working together can create.

And to **Bob Bashor**, a new friend, who helped me find the deepest meanings in the things I was trying to say and who both evoked and provoked some of the best this book has to offer.

The help they provided goes far beyond what was singled out here. They were my colleagues, sisters, and brothers on this pioneering journey. And Savannah, you are the light of my life.

There are many others I want to thank. Several of them and their pioneering visions are described in Chapter 2. Stories about many others are scattered throughout the book. I would like to take the time here to thank a few others.

Tom McNamee provided helpful praise and rigorous critique of the manuscript. Tom's suggestions were the most useful I have ever received. Leah Mathison provided valuable research, good editorial sense, fine organizational development instincts, and the hot tip that something special might be going on at Vignette. My friend and colleague Geoff Bellman, whose presence and wise counsel nurtures my soul, read and made suggestions for the manuscript. Marl Yeoell read the first draft and provided many helpful suggestions. Reed Whittle gave many organizational development insights, as well as sound personal understanding. Beth Summers provided very helpful guidance early in the process and helped clarify the meaning of pioneering. Karena Senchack provided encouragement and inspiration for my first efforts at describing what I was seeing; many of her special insights are scattered throughout this book. And Oscar Mink and Claire Weinstein, both inspirational teachers and loyal friends, contributed to my understanding of organizations and of human learning. Herb Rogers of Lockheed expanded my understanding and appreciation of employee involvement. And I would like to thank Fredric Margolis, a consultant's consultant, for his many insights.

I would particularly like to recognize the efforts of the people at Executive Excellence Publishing—Megan Vandre for her gifted editing, Ken Shelton for seeing the promise in this book, Calvin Harper, Jim Easley, and Ted Hartman for their help. They made this a much better book.

I want to recognize the profound impact of two pioneering organizations that continue to carry a torch that brings light to human minds and fire for their spirits. One is Plan II, a pioneering liberal arts program at the University of Texas, and the other is the Harry Ransom Humanities Research Center. Plan II is in the tradition of the great liberal arts programs of European, British, and Ivy League universities. The Humanities Research Center is one of the two greatest collections of rare books and original manuscripts and writings in the world. I particularly want to thank a number of people associated with those institutions who challenged me, inspired me, introduced me to the great ideas of the world—the best thinking from all fields of knowledge—and planted in me an unending thirst for learning and for the truth.

My special thanks to John Silber who taught me the importance of the combat of ideas, but who also showed me his compassion. John Silber is one of the great individualists of his time, and his passion for social justice has involved him far more than most academics in the affairs of the world. I want to thank Irwin Spear for his personal interest in my writing and for the passion with which he taught biology. Irwin's vision simply danced the sacredness of living systems. I have many warm memories of the late Willis Pratt, whose quiet, romantic passion for great poetry and prose revealed the high intention and eternal hopes for human civilization. And I also remember that giant in economics, the late institutional economist Clarence Ayres, one of John Kenneth Galbraith's teachers, who eloquently and accurately forecast the coming age when business would by necessity work for economic fairness and the sharing of prosperity. Finally, I would like to thank Harry Ransom, an exuberant individualist and pioneering thinker. My participation as a student in the '60's (before the demonstrations) on his trailblazing student advisory committee led me to a career in trying to make a difference in the institutions that get things done in this world.

Thanks to Ray Bard, who believed in me the first time. The success of that early book in many ways paved the way for this one. I appreciate the special support provided by Warren Cullar and Kitty Biel in the hard early stages of the writing. Thanks to Diane Davis, who collaborated on many of the ideas that resulted in the principles of communication and trust. When I was in the middle of the first draft, Diane also showed me a view from the mountain tops that lifted my vision. To Jim Beerstecher, a talented, resourceful, and caring man: thanks for your friendship and support. Thanks to Dawn Rosch for sticking by me on so many occasions. Thanks to Kitty Smith and her partners at Central City Builders, whose vision is to build fine, new homes in inner city neighborhoods where people can live without adding to the congestion, pollution, and road rage that comes from long-distance commuting. Kitty is a friend for all seasons and all conditions, who listens to my doubts and concerns and offers well-placed, candid advice.

I would also like to thank Tim and Barbara Cook and the folks at The Church of Conscious Harmony for giving me the "eyes" to see and the heart to understand. As Tim says, "Loving your neighbor is such a simple idea, but very difficult to do. You have to find the real 'I' in you first and see your own contradictions and hidden motives. Then you may have enough compassion to begin to learn how to love." Thanks particularly to Sharon Clark for the many hours of sharing, soul searching, and unflinching truth. I would like to thank Linda Pendegrass, the minister at Unity of Austin, for the understanding of Jesus' vision and example of leadership. Thanks also to Jake Shelley, a light in the Methodist Church, for my early spiritual understandings. Thank you to the men and women who participated with me in the pioneering vision called Communities Rising, particularly Hal Chesner and Junius and Malia Johnson. Malia's current vision is to use cable television to teach the knowledge of nursing to those ordinary people in rural America who must provide home care for their elderly, far from the medical resources of cities.

I would like to thank the Bozemans and the Davises, who were my strong family roots growing up and the people of the then small rural town of Plano, Texas, for their many lessons of community and individualism. And I would particularly like to thank my principal at Plano High School, Bill Williams, for the freedom to move around; Mrs. Frost, who first recognized my individualism; and my two English teachers, Mrs. Hardison and Mrs. Skaggs, for a firm foundation of writing skills.

Thank you also to Mama Bozeman, who was the wisest person I ever met. I hope a little of it rubbed off on me. Also, "Uncle" Foy Lemons, for us getting our heads together about the matters of this world when I was a boy of seven. My Aunt Ruby, for her warm kitchen and conversations as I grew up. My Uncle Tucker, who spent hours showing this boy how to do things; it's very important to know how to do things. My Aunt Nellie, who introduced me to the wonders of the big city and always made me feel like I was special, just as she made my 13 other cousins feel special too, and after that my son and stepsons. And her husband Ed, who is one of the kindest, most generous men I've ever known. I would like to thank my three stepchildren, Michael, John, and Angela for sharing their lives, their fears and their dreams. You made my life enormously richer. And I would especially like to thank my sister Lynn, for not resenting her big brother's shadow and for always being understanding and loving even when at times I was not behaving well.

Finally, I would like to give a big thanks to the more than 1,000 women and men who worked with me in the trenches of all of these organizations, revealing their fears and concerns, but more important, their hopes, fine intentions, high visions, and courage to take risks to make their organizations better places to work and better at serving the needs of their customers and their communities.

To all of you, this book is your gift to me. I hope it is our gift to the world.

—Larry Davis

Contents

Foreword

December 25, 1955, was a red-letter day in my life. Santa must have thought I had been a very good boy. Under the Christmas tree was a genuine Davy Crockett coonskin cap, a gift many boys got that year due to the "top of the charts" popularity of Tennessee Ernie Ford's rendition of "The Ballad of Davy Crockett."

But I got more! Not only did I get the coveted cap with its coon's tail hanging down, but Santa brought me a genuine Davy Crockett air rifle (we called them BB guns back then). It even had a brass ring and a long leather tong on the side, just like the "ol' Betsy" that Davy had. With that hat and BB gun, I *was* "king of the wild frontier."

Davy was my hero. Davy was a pioneer. I mean, he was a "born on the mountain top in Tennessee, raised in the woods so he knew every tree, killed him a bar (bear) when he was only three" type pioneer. Long before Christmas dinner was served, I had headed for the woods near my South Georgia home in search of a "bar," and with the rugged individualism I knew Davy had. No sisters were allowed; in fact, you went it alone. Being Davy Crockett was decidedly a solo act!

For many years to follow, I held the belief that true pioneers were all like Davy: courageous, visionary, and primarily solitary. You never heard of the Kroc brothers, the Ford brothers, or the Edison brothers! Pioneers may have traveled with groups, but I was convinced their orientation had to be solo. Pioneering was *not* a group thing.

Then I moved to Texas. Standing on the sacred ground of the Alamo in San Antonio, I learned about the real Davy Crockett. He was visionary all right, but it was a shared vision, one blended with others yearning for a free Texas. He was courageous. But it was a consolidated bravery inspired by the team commitment of several hundred men willing to sacrifice everything against obvious and overwhelming odds.

Davy was by no means alone. The Alamo was about a collective stand for a valued cause. Leadership was less about rank and more about soul. Eyewitness Enrique Esparza said it this way: "Crockett seemed to be the leading spirit. He was everywhere. Colonel [William B.] Travis was chief in command, but he depended more upon the judgment of Crockett and that brave man's coolness than upon his own" (quoted in the *San Antonio Express*, May 12, 1907). Bottom line, there was no greater expression of pioneering than that shouted from the stone walls of a tiny mission during a cold, two-week period in early 1836. As the words "Remember the Alamo" spread, the event became a flame that ignited patriotic passion throughout an emerging new country.

We live in a time when the soul of enterprise is in the midst of transformation. Most organizations are in a battle for survival, and their very nature is under attack. The word *organized* has historically been synonymous with order, control, and predictability. Leaders of the past were not expected to be courageous. In fact, mavericks were a threat to the fabric of organization. Sure, they fared well in small entrepreneurial ventures; however, let that venture expand a bit and suddenly accounting replaced daring; caution supplanted bravery. And creativity? It was only reserved for R&D and advertising, certainly not for the buttoned-down, starched executives enthroned on mahogany row.

The advent of the Internet and related technology, coupled with intense global competition and a growing number of employees who are more interested in purpose than promotion, has created conditions for metamorphosis. Managers today speak of iconoclastic Disney and flamboyant Southwest Airlines in the same reverent manner they once reserved for white-shirt IBM and somber General Motors. Empowerment is debated as heatedly as earnings per share. Concepts like "culture," "self-directed teams," "diversity," and "telecommuting" now pepper the conversations at the top of the organization.

Many organizations continue to cling to their comfortable old style; their few modifications are mostly in form only. They issue "empowerment policies" instead of empowering. Or they appoint a "czar of diversity" and label themselves progressive. Other organizations, recognizing that incrementalism is the path to extinction, are opting for a complete abandonment of classical organization in pursuit of individualism. "Virtual" means a network of mercenaries. Outsourcing replaces loyalty. Employment contracts are in; solemn pledges are out. Flat is good; pyramid is bad. Business casual is an attitude as well as a type of attire.

Absent from this contest between plain-vanilla organization and egotistical individualism has been a relevant field description of effective leadership. Until now. *Pioneering Organizations* provides a new framework for helping enterprises combine the synergy of the team with the conviction of the individual. It offers leaders a deeply grounded philosophy and practice of how to galvanize vision, unearth spirit, and channel courage in a fashion that forges contribution. Larry Davis challenges leaders to passionately pursue cause, to communicate with authenticity, and to embrace great teamwork as the manifestation of aligned individualism.

Davy Crockett held no official position at the Battle of the Alamo. His legacy is such that history books describe him as a person who engendered trust and inspired passion. As Colonel Jim Bowie wrote in a letter to Governor Henry Smith, "Davy Crockett has been animating the men to do their duty."

The new millennium is shaping up to be a wild frontier. And organizations that thrive in the wild will be those led by pioneer leaders who understand that at its bedrock foundation, leadership is the process of *"animating* people to do their duty."

—Chip R. Bell, author of *Customer Love,*
Customers as Partners and co-author of *Beep! Beep!*
Competing in the Age of the Roadrunner

Introduction

S tarting a new company is a ludicrous idea. You start out with absolutely nothing. Right away, you need absolutely everything. The set of things under your direct control is quite small. The set of things that can cause you to fail is infinite. The set of extremely difficult things that must get done right away is large (not quite infinite, but still very large). Even the simplest tasks can be a problem just because there are so many of them—no matter how much you've done and how far along you are, something trivial seems always to stand between you and what you really want to get done.

My favorite example of this is the first coffee machine at Vignette. Neither Ross Garber nor I drink much coffee, and as it turns out, neither did the first few employees we hired. Not surprisingly, there was no coffee machine in the office. It never occurred to us that we had overlooked anything in the "office necessities" category. When we finally hired someone with a serious coffee habit, he showed up at the office and the first thing he said was, "What do you mean you don't have any coffee here?" So before we could make much progress, we had to go out and buy a coffee machine (we also hadn't hired an office manager yet—another thing that was on the to-be-done list). Buying a coffee machine wasn't hard, of course, but the point is that even the easy things are a substantial obstacle to a new company's success simply because there are so many "easy" things that have to be done.

Ross and I had a general understanding of the odds against us. Both of us had been in and around a number of start-ups throughout our careers. Both of us had seen examples of successes and examples of failures, and we were quite familiar with the risks and issues. One of the important things you learn from experience is that there are many things you have no control over; you just have to live with those risks. Yes, you can have contingency plans and grand strategies, but if you are honest with yourself you will realize that some things just happen as they happen.

On the other hand, we also knew there were quite a few things we did control. With so much uncertainty in a start-up, we wanted to make sure we found all the things we could control and made the most of them. I believed that one of the largest success factors we could control (or at least influence), and one most companies overlook (or get wrong), would be the relationship between Vignette and its employees. Anyone in the technology workforce has seen examples of misguided corporate policies and has witnessed the powerfully negative and destructive effects that silly policies can have on employee morale and productivity. As a case in point, Scott Adams' Dilbert comic strip is funny precisely because it is so pathetically true. But I wondered how we could harness this powerful effect as a positive force instead of a destructive force. Surely there had to be a way to align everyone's interests so employees and managers automatically and naturally did what was best for both the company and themselves.

It was that sort of thinking that led us to many of the decisions we made in starting and managing Vignette. For example, I wanted to make sure the employees we hired didn't waste money (because we had very little money in the beginning). I was not fond of the traditional solutions to this problem, which mostly seemed to consist of making a purchasing process that was so arcane and restrictive that no employees would be able to figure out how to *spend* any money at all, let alone *waste* any. In fact, I worked in a company like this once. Engineers needed diskettes on a regular basis, but no one could even figure out how to navigate through the procurement maze in the company. Instead, we would buy the floppies at the computer store and find some other way to get the company "back" for the money it "owed" us.

My solution to achieving fiscal responsibility in the early days of Vignette was much simpler. Each time we interviewed a candidate, I told him or her how much venture capital we had raised, how much money we still had in the bank, and on what day the paychecks would begin bouncing. My goal was to align their natural, individualistic ideas with our vision, which in this case was to get the first product out the door before we ran out of money. By leading the employees in an open, forthright fashion, I did more to crystallize the importance of spending the company's money in a responsible way than any 51-page purchasing policy manual ever could. And this technique unleashed powerful creative forces as well. We had employees finding all sorts of resourceful ways to save money (something that would never come from the dictatorial purchasing policy manual approach).

We generalized this concept into something we called an "adult environment," by which we meant that we treated our employees like adults, not like children. We always strove to give them as much information as possible and to treat them with the respect they deserved. One way we did this was by holding *open*, weekly executive staff meetings. I'm talking about those weekly meetings where the CEO and senior staff get together and discuss various week-to-week operational issues. My experience as a "grunt" has been that employees usually attach some mystical aura to these meetings. "What's going on behind those closed doors?" they ask. Frankly, if you've ever been in one of those meetings, you know they are usually pretty dull and routine. But still, with all the executives in a room for hours with the door closed, people can't help but wonder what nefarious things might be going on in there. I wanted to eliminate that "us" vs. "them" feeling between employees and management, and even more important, I wanted to make sure our employees got some insight into what it really took to grow and run our business.

To accomplish this goal, I set up a program where employees could sign up to attend an executive staff meeting as an observer. Three interesting things happened from this experiment. First, the "observer" idea didn't last long. Starting with the first meeting and in almost every meeting thereafter, the "observer" became a participant and contributed valuable perspectives and ideas to the meetings. Second, we never had to ask an employee to leave while we discussed sensitive material. We trusted our employees, and any time a sensitive topic came up, we simply asked them to treat the confidential information appropriately. We never had a single instance of an employee abusing this trust. Third, as more and more employees had their chance to participate in the meeting, you could feel the mutual respect grow as employees got a better understanding of what "those executive guys" really did.

These days, obviously, as we've grown larger, the specific management tricks we used when we were small don't always apply any more. Some things we used to do, such as sharing sales pipeline and revenue data, are actually prohibited by law or regulation now that we are a public company. So we don't hold open executive staff meetings, and we don't post interim financials in the cafeteria. But the general principle still applies—we look for ways to solve problems by getting everyone's interests aligned; we look for ways to share information and engage our employees; and we are careful about the secondary signals our actions send. As companies grow larger, it has been my experience that these secondary signals are actually a much more powerful form of communication than the mere words the management team utters at company meetings.

Pioneering Organizations is about all of these things. It is about the forces behind the Vignette fiscal responsibility anecdote and the open executive meeting anecdote, as well as many similar stories that have unfolded throughout industries. It is about the signals leaders send to their teams and how to get everyone's interests converging in a way that will unleash levels of productivity and, well, pioneering that most organizations can only dream of. Larry Davis is on to something here, something Ross and I were doing by the seat of our pants without an explicit understanding of exactly why what we were doing worked. This book impressed me because it provides the "whys" and also many of the "hows." I found that its topics resonated with many of my experiences.

Pioneering Organizations will change the way you think about management techniques, organizational structures, and the dynamics of building successful teams and companies. It will help you think like an industry pioneer.

—Neil Webber, co-founder of the Vignette Corporation

Preface

*I*n every age, a few organizations rise above all others. They answer the call to move forward, to risk the unknown, to find the needed answers, to break down the barriers of their time. These pioneering organizations open new possibilities for all humankind. They make possible the lives we live each day. We eat, drink, work, play, and sleep with the aid of their creations. They establish the leading edge of the human adventure.

These organizations are exciting places to work, full of energy, hope, faith, conviction, and incredible degrees of commitment and loyalty. The people who work in them believe they are on a quest to "bring fire" to humanity. This book explores the forces that converge to create pioneering organizations and to energize their ascendance. It also examines the reasons for their decline. Based on this analysis, it identifies the factors that must exist to develop and sustain pioneering organizations.

The book will help you gain a new understanding of organizations and of certain primal forces operating within them. Until now, these forces, which are largely unseen and unspoken, yet pivotal in determining success or failure, have gone strangely unnoticed and unexplored. As a result, many organizational "solutions" fail, or are only partially successful. But extraordinary accomplishments sometimes happen "naturally," even when everything seems stacked against them. And this book helps explain why some small renegade bands occasionally pull off miracles.

The paradigms are changing. Today, rational management practices sometimes drive organizations into the ground. And resistance to certain kinds of change and change management is growing. As someone put it, "People are so damned tired of inspiring vision statements and consultant tricks, while management is whistling on the way to the bank, that they just want to raise a little hell." There are no trick plays in this book.

Leadership has been a popular topic of management literature for the past 50 years. Teamwork has been a best-selling topic for more than a decade. In the latter half of the 19th century, individualism was in vogue, both as a concept and as an explanation of organizational success. But these are more than just topics. They are pivotal organizational forces. We know each of them is powerfully influential in determining organizational success or failure, yet the *interaction* of them has been little studied and less understood. These factors are the *primary* forces operating within organizations, and their dynamic interaction is the key to organizational effectiveness. When these forces converge, they produce high-performing organizations. When the vision is about breakthrough results that can benefit all, the convergence of these forces provides the extraordinary energy and determination that powers pioneering organizations.

In today's world, various ideas stand in the way of convergence. Individualism is not the same thing as the "me-ism" of the '80s or the bull market of the '90s. Teamwork is not confined to some mystical abstraction or groundless noun called a "team"; it is in fact the essence of organization. "Empowerment," particularly the human resources fantasy version of it, has invited an epidemic of soured attitudes, immobilized supervisors, and made teamwork more difficult than ever. The team fad, particularly the "self-directed" strain of it, sometimes nets wide-scale cynicism, and the "team loyalty test" often produces fear and resentment in otherwise healthy, well-adjusted people. A "team player" spirit sometimes whips up a fervor of peer group bonding that raises barriers between groups rather than lowering them, while generating no measurably better results from the team or for the organization.

A great deal of leadership practice and theory is still too much about control, compliance, manipulation, and even deception. Organizational theory and organizational development have often been little better. Many of these practices, however, are not a matter of bad intentions, but of poor understanding. Organizational understanding has been dominated by partial, unrelated theories—theories that treated individualism, teamwork, and leadership as independent variables. As one result, individualism, once revered, has been progressively discouraged over the past 50 years. In more recent times, it is even being suppressed. This book argues that individualism, in its highest form, is the source of organizational power and brilliance.

What I am advocating is a strong convergence of individualism and teamwork—teamwork built on healthy self-interest—and leadership that encourages and integrates the contributions of both. While the roots of this idea go back at least to the Magna Carta, this interdependent balancing of the interests of the individual with those of the group and community may have been the secret of pioneer America's economic success. The U.S. Constitution was carefully crafted to create such a balance. Today, when global success should be our goal, this convergent balance is even more important. Individualism tied to teamwork creates a dynamic tension that explains the energy and industry of pioneering cultures. It is an accelerator for extraordinary action. It may be a key to prosperity for all.

More than 25 years of organizational development consulting with every level of every kind of organization, led me to the conviction that most organizations can rise to pioneering levels and achieve the extraordinary performance that comes with pioneering and convergence. This conviction grew from seeing the amazing results that some rather simple processes achieved in ordinary organizations. The results occurred time and time again. And it was not my experience only, but that of many of my colleagues. Simple processes of involvement, respect, and a search for solutions that work for all yielded results far beyond anything that could have been expected. There must be more to it than the process. These processes must be tapping something primal and powerful. Something that, when tapped, sets off a chain reaction.

This book reports results and provides an analysis of the factors that produced breakthroughs. Part I presents the principles behind those breakthroughs: the special magic of pioneering visions; the intricate weave of interests into a convergence that forges commitment; the conditions that support the development of healthy, interdependent individualism; the kinds of agreements required for true teamwork; and the leadership practices that bring people together with fire in their nostrils to do the impossible. Part II provides the "how to"—the charts, maps, navigational tools, processes, and situational examples needed to begin the pioneering journey. Success in the future will require nothing less than companies that can truly innovate both externally and internally. It will require pioneers. This book can help you get there, and I believe you will enjoy the adventure.

AN EXPLORATION INTO PIONEERING ORGANIZATIONS

In every age, there exist those organizations that rise to the challenge of their times. They see a way to bring a gift to the world that will meet pressing needs or solve difficult problems. They see a way to expand the possibilities of human life. They are not deterred by predictions of failure, but are drawn forward by hope. They are energized by faith and commitment and sustained by seemingly inexhaustible spirit. Often, their dreams seem impossible. But those who succeed give us our very lives.

Part 1 explores the source of power in pioneering visions. It examines how pioneering visions achieve a powerful convergence of people and resources that carries organizations through. It describes the characteristics of the exceptional individuals who make pioneering ideas happen—those independent-thinking people who commit to the vision and will not give up. This section presents the principles that underlie unprecedented levels of teamwork, as well as the kind of leadership it takes to accomplish what leaders of other organizations cannot even imagine. It is about rethinking the way we conduct our businesses and our lives every day to determine whether our practices now will lead the efforts of the future.

Pioneering Organizations

P ioneering . . . To sail off bravely into the unknown. To discover new lands. To overcome overwhelming obstacles and incredible odds. To create amazing new technologies. To find fresh solutions to old problems. To meet the challenge wherever it may be. To keep going and never give up or turn back. These are just a few of the meanings of the word *pioneering*.

History is rich with stories of pioneering women and men. Their exploits thrill and inspire us. They make possible the lives we live each day. We walk on the ground they discovered. We eat, drink, work, play, and sleep with the aid of their creations. We live longer and healthier lives because of the diseases they cured. Our minds are full of their insights. Our emotions are stirred by their words and their faith. Our imaginations are filled with visions that their breakthroughs made possible. Throughout history, they have answered the call to move forward. They establish the leading edge of the human adventure.

Across the years, there have also been a scattering of pioneering organizations—organizations that somehow saw it as their mission to open the way for the rest of us. These organizations were exciting places to work, full of energy, hope, faith, belief, and incredible degrees of commitment and loyalty. The people who worked in them felt they were part of a quest to "bring fire" to humanity. They knew that if they advanced, the world would cheer.

In our time, there was NASA's Mercury program and later "one small step for man, one giant leap for mankind." In the 1950s, the efforts of the organizations seeking the secrets of semiconductors and the quantum condensation of microcircuitry pioneered the Information Age. And more recently, we have found our lives forever altered by organizations engineering the World Wide Web and launching our minds into cyberspace.

At some point, many of today's large corporations were pioneering organizations: Ford, IBM, Bell, General Electric, Boeing, American Airlines. That was how they got large. As a young college intern, I personally witnessed the early pioneering days at Texas Instruments; the transistor was just beginning to change the world, and integrated circuits were on the drawing board. At Texas Instruments' Central Research Laboratories, a wireless world was being envisioned. Apple had its pioneering days, as did Nike, Microsoft, Southwest Airlines, and Intel. Today, Dell, Cisco Systems, Starbucks, Amazon.com, and the Vignette Corporation can make a claim to that title. And the Whole Foods Markets, The Post Ranch Inn, Classic Communications, and Kinko's have also pioneered new possibilities for their markets.

Sometimes it is a part of a larger organization that catches the pioneering spirit and leads the way. The Bell Labs of the 1950s comes to mind. Or the Lockheed team that in World War II designed a winning bomber over a weekend. Or the IC^2 Institute at the University of Texas that catalyzed a wave of technology commercialization in Austin that has crested with it as one of the hottest IT, internet, and e-commerce cities in the world.

These examples show that pioneering takes many forms. But the form is not important. What is crucial is that without pioneering, we will cease to move forward, facing and solving the challenges of our time. As an ancient Eastern philosopher said in the Bhagavad Gita, "If I did not work, these worlds would perish." I believe that. I also believe that without pioneering—without those who seek a way to move ahead—these worlds will perish. Given the compression of the global community with its many problems and opportunities, nothing less than pioneering will serve 21st century humankind and the organizations on which we all depend.

For reasons that have been little understood, the pioneering phase passes. Camelot is lost. This book identifies some of the reasons. More usefully, it identifies the factors that must exist for pioneering organizations to develop in the first place and for them to endure. A primary factor is that they must have a pioneering vision—a burning passion for an achievement that opens new possibilities for all humankind. But that is not enough. Many start-up ventures have pioneering visions, but fail to bring them to fruition. Pioneering organizations must also move beyond the traditional conflict that results from some people's interests being served at the expense of others' and achieve a convergence of interests that serves the needs and purposes of all.

Another crucial factor found in pioneering organizations is choice—individual human choice, the unbowed choice we call individualism. But it must be a form of individualism that knows its interdependence. Such individuals are the source of both innovation and commitment. Due to the complexity of work and of systems, pioneering organizations today also call for the highest levels of teamwork in history. Many of the recent concepts about teams, however, are ultimately counterproductive. What is required is a kind of teamwork that can be seen as aligned individualism. Finally, pioneering organizations require a particular form of leadership— leadership in the interests of all. Only this kind of leadership can achieve a convergence of interests that holds up under fire.

These five factors are the subject of Part 1 of this book, but to begin, let's explore them briefly here.

A PIONEERING VISION

The extraordinary levels of energy, effort, and faith found in pioneering organizations are fueled by the vision of what those in the organization expect to do together. This vision acts like a beacon, drawing forth the best from those involved. All collectively held visions are powerful organizational motivators, but a pioneering vision taps longings deep in the human soul, releasing a force that can perform miracles. Yes, pioneering is about doing something that has never been done before—pushing the edge of the envelope, as Chuck Yeager, the record-breaking test pilot, put it—but not just for glory or profit. In pioneering, there is the sense that the hard-won breakthrough is *for us all*. Somehow, pioneers are drawn to challenge barriers that are perceived to be the limits of human possibility. What they achieve will then become possible for others.

For example, when Roger Bannister first broke the four-minute mile, it completely changed the world's view of how fast human beings could run. That freed the energy and muscles of others to run even faster. And the principle is the same for all pioneering. Every true breakthrough leads to another. If Bannister had not broken that record, would anyone have bothered to invent a better running shoe? Would Nike have challenged the world to "Just Do It"?

Henry Ford provides another good example of a pioneering vision. His vision, as historian Daniel J. Boorstin put it, was to "build a motor car for the great multitude. ... It will be so low in price that no man making a good salary will be unable to own one—and enjoy with his family the blessing of hours of pleasure in God's great open spaces."[1]

A CONVERGENCE OF INTERESTS

Typically, organizations serve some interests at the expense of others. This sets up an inherent conflict within them, limiting innovation and commitment. The reason this is so disabling is embedded in the very nature of the entities known as organizations. Organizations can be defined as people working together to achieve certain purposes. They work best when the purposes are both *mutual* and *reciprocal*. It is a mistake to believe that organizations exist for a single purpose—to serve the needs of their customers or to create profits for their owners. All organizations have a multiplicity of purposes, the two just mentioned, to be sure. But just as important are the interests of the individuals and teams that work within organizations. Less directly, the interests of the communities that support and are supported by organizations need to also be served. In the broadest sense, perhaps, humanity itself must be served—or at least not disserved.

In many organizations, the fashionable efforts to develop a sense of "ownership" in employees are manipulative. If employees do not own stock in a company, they are not the owners. If they do not own significant stock, they are not influential owners. Their interests, however, still need to be served. That involves such things as interesting and developmental work that does not injure them and appropriate compensation for serving the interests of the organization and its customers. Yes, it is better when employees also believe in the organization's purpose, but for any organization to be effective, employees must at least believe that their interests are being served. We must stop making *self-interest* a bad word. After all, self-interest has continued to be rewarded for CEOs and other top managers. It may involve less money, but it is no less important to the secretary or the factory worker.

Pioneering organizations, the ones that truly lead in our world, achieve a true convergence of all of these interests. Everything that such organizations do is designed to simultaneously serve the desires and needs of everyone involved and everyone impacted. At the Vignette Corporation, that is precisely what Neil Webber and Ross Garber, its founders, set out to do. They designed the *kind* of organization they wanted to work in and only then did market research to determine what *product* their organization would make. Their success, the spirit of their employees, and the feel of the place as you walk down the halls looking into offices, conference rooms, and the customer training center, indicate they have achieved just such a convergence. At the Post Ranch Inn on the Big Sur of California, Mike Freed, Billy Post, and Larry Callahan have created a profitable and magical convergence beneficial to guests, local artisans, employees, and the preservation of the planet earth. At Starbucks, the convergence created by Howard Shultz's innovative compensation and benefit plans for part-time employees has admirably served the interests of employees, investors, and a huge following of loyal customers, making it one of the fastest growing businesses in the world.

A complete convergence of interests forms a firm foundation for individual commitment and true teamwork. In its highest form, it is a kind of interdependent interaction that causes all purposes to be experienced as mutual purposes. Such a convergence, at least for a time, is part of what makes pioneering organizations so powerful. Everyone involved is committed to the vision *and to each other.* They feel like they are part of, belong to, and count in achieving that vision. Pioneering organizations set the standard for others to follow. The loss of convergence or the manipulation of some interests in behalf of others can also be one of the reasons that the pioneering spirit leaves an organization.

INTERDEPENDENT INDIVIDUALISM

Try to imagine pioneering without individualism. Traditionally, individualism has meant the ability to have an independent point of view, the willingness to act independently in service of that point of view, and a high degree of self-reliance. But I think it has also always been defined by a strong sense of community and a desire to make a contribution. Individualism clears the path for new possibilities for the human race. What would our world have been without a Galileo to question the nature of the universe?

It is important to distinguish individualism from mere eccentricity, alternate lifestyles, or other efforts to be different for the sake of being different. It must also not be confused with the isolationism of a hermit. Individualism is engaged. Furthermore, individualism does not refer to the views of those not in touch with reality, whether those views are due to mental illness or merely due to fantasy. Individualism has a strong sense of what is real and of the possibilities that are inherent within reality. The recent disassociated actions of teenage killers are not a form of individualism. On the contrary, they are the acts of peer-referenced, dependent boys who feel the insecurity of not being able to fit in. They are not the confi-dent actions of people with independence of thought.

Perhaps most important, individualism must not be associated with mere selfishness, the self-focused and self-absorbed "me-ism" of the '80s, for example. Individualism is an intense effort to under-stand, to find one's own answers. In its developed and mature forms, individualism is a quest for the truth and a search for better ways of doing things. These "better ways" usually contain seeds of self-interest, but when they are coupled with visions of how others will be better served as well, they fulfill the concept of "enlightened self-interest." The term I am using for this is *interdependent individu-alism*. Henry Ford's vision, quoted above, is a good example of self-interests interwoven with service.

Here are a few modern examples. At Classic Communications, CEO Merritt Belisle encourages an environment in which every indi-vidual can question whether or not its "emperor" is "wearing clothes." He regularly asks employees what their first priority would be if they were CEO for a day. At the Whole Foods Markets, individ-ualism in lifestyle was welcomed from the first. It is a hallmark of both its employees and its customers. Employee ideas have always been the basis for a large part of its stores' business strategies.

Every form of pioneering described above starts with a desire for better possibilities. For it to go beyond desire, however, individuals must be willing to break out of the conventional wisdom of their time and to alienate their contemporaries, if necessary. While pio-neering often involves a group and includes peer support, at its inception it requires the independent thinking and choice of at least one individual with a vision. Pioneering depends on individualism.

TEAMWORK AS ALIGNED INDIVIDUALISM

The complexity of work and of systems in organizations today calls for the highest levels of teamwork in history. Many of the recent concepts about teams, however, are ultimately counterproductive. This book argues for teamwork, not teams. Work is organized in sys-tems that cross many teams, not as discreet tasks for work units.

Consequently, strengthening teams often results in stronger boundaries between units, and therefore in tougher turf protection. Strong unit teams may result in production gains within those units, but frequently produce a net loss across the entire system due to conflicts between the teams. Teamwork throughout systems and in all directions is what is needed.

The strongest examples I have seen of this kind of teamwork take the form of aligned individualism, not peer bonding. Individualists, intent on getting something done, will commit totally to a plan of action once it is agreed to, but that is usually after intense debate about the actions to be taken, not after personal sharing. The behaviors for this kind of teamwork are not what has been called for in many training sessions on teams. The needed behaviors are not about understanding our personality or cultural differences. They are about surfacing and resolving differences of opinion about the work to be done. When people focus fully on what to do or how best to do it together, they tend to go blind to personality and cultural preferences.

The behaviors of effective teamwork are also not primarily about being sensitive. It is, of course, important to be sensitive, but the main attention must be focused on figuring out how to help each other do what is needed to get the job done and to reach the intended goals. This kind of teamwork *is sensitive* to what is required to serve the interests of employees, as well as those of the customer, organization, and shareholders, but it is not particularly interested in people's emotional baggage. Its sensitivity is to the system as a whole and to the contributions needed from and for both the individuals and the teams comprising the system.

A very good example of this kind of teamwork occurred at Abbott Labs a few years back. A cross-functional group of mechanics, operators, and engineers found a way to solve a seven-year-old problem in production. Each of these functional groups was represented by some strong, blunt-speaking individualists. Initially, they were quite direct in stating what they thought the other groups were doing wrong. But they also listened, finally adopting many actions that had been opposed by their peer groups. Their teamwork was so successful that production increased by more than 60 percent. Not only did the company benefit, but their functional teams ended up benefiting as well. This is also true at Collective Technologies, where the entire business strategy is built around the teamwork of entrepreneurial individualists.

CONVERGENT LEADERSHIP

In a real sense, all pioneering efforts are led by a vision, not just by a charismatic leader. Pioneering leaders live a passion for that vision. Often, they are the individualist visionaries themselves— Edison for example. But sometimes, as it may have been in some of the more famous high-tech efforts, they are leaders who catch the vision and have the ability to bring people together in passionate service of it. When pioneering leaders are putting together an organization, there is an intuitive awareness that the interests of all must be served. Ego and power sometimes take over, however, and leaders start to imagine that they alone are important to the success of the venture; they begin to ignore the interests of those actually doing the work. Ultimately, this leads to failure of the venture or a decline in the pioneering spirit that drives it.

The world needs a new kind of leadership, one that is consciously aware of and committed to serving the interests of all involved. Merritt Belisle and Steven Seach at Classic Communications have minds that work that way. In the course of a half-hour meeting, they are likely to concern themselves with customer service, the needs of the employees, shareholder and investor profits, community service projects for the small towns the company serves, the latest technologies in the industry, incentives for their managers, ways Classic Communications can make living in rural America more viable, and ways to help a colleague shave strokes off his golf game. Convergent leadership works to assure that organizations serve all such needs simultaneously. At the Post Ranch Inn, the attention that the organization gives to supporting employees in solving problems in their personal lives and the lives of their families and communities (not just their problems at work), is a major factor in the level of customer service those employees provide. People helping people is infectious.

Convergent leadership is required to develop pioneering organizations, and given the complexity and competition of the 21st century, it will be required to sustain them. This kind of leadership, which I call chieftain leadership, is not truly new. It has served humanity well in its tribal forms, and it was commonplace in the pioneering organizations mentioned above. Given the theory and practice of leadership in recent times, however, such leadership will not only seem new, it will seem pioneering.

A Pioneering
Vision

Super Bowl XVIII in 1984 was nearly eclipsed by a dramatic computer ad that stirred the soul and made people want to stand up and shout. When the black, white, and gray image of society was shattered by the exciting, colorful world of Macintosh computers to come, viewers wanted to join the revolution in any way they could. Many did, buying up Macintosh computers as fast as they hit the stores.

Beth Summers, a group HR manager for Apple at the time, described the scene when Apple employees were first shown that ad a few weeks before the game. They cheered! They jumped up and down! They went wild! They did not see it as hype, as typical TV commercial exaggeration. They knew it was true. They knew they would do it!

That is the power of a pioneering vision. It stirs the soul. It galvanizes action. It rallies people to perform extraordinary feats. "I have a dream," said Martin Luther King. And John F. Kennedy said, "We will put a man on the moon by the end of this decade," and "Ask not what your country can do for you; ask what you can do for your country." These visions set thousands marching for civil rights, enlisted a dedicated band into service through the Peace Corps, and sent test pilots, scientists, and teachers rocketing into space. Many more were moved by other words and other visions. What is the attraction?

All of these have been heralded as examples of the power of vision. And they are that, but they are more. They are *pioneering* visions. That is their special power. Let's consider each of those words.

VISION

The word *vision* not only describes a remarkable human capacity, but it also embraces several different levels of that capacity. The first level could simply be called seeing, but usually means *seeing what is there that is hidden to others*. It is this level of vision that spiritual writing refers to as the "light of the soul." It might also be described as being able to see the "now" moment. Perhaps the most moving description of such vision is in Teilhard de Chardin's *The Phenomenon of Man*:

> *Seeing*. We might say that the whole of life lies in that verb—if not ultimately, at least essentially. Fuller being is closer union: such is the kernel and conclusion of this book. But let us emphasize the point: union increases only through an increase in consciousness, that is to say in vision. And that, doubtless, is why the history of the living world can be summarized as the elaboration of ever more perfect eyes within a cosmos in which there is always more to be seen. After all, do we not judge the perfection of an animal or the supremacy of a thinking being by the penetration and synthetic power of its gaze? To try to see more and better is not a matter of whim or curiosity or self-indulgence. *To see or to perish* is the very condition laid upon everything that makes up the universe, by reason of the mysterious gift of existence. And this, in superior measure, is man's condition.[2]

The second level of vision could be called *seeing what is not there*, or at least what is not there in present reality. The oldest form of vision at this level is the ability to see the future—the gift of prophets, oracles, and shamen. The most discussed recent form is the ability to see desirable futures—the gift attributed to great leaders in business, science, or government. By implication, this ability refers to being able to see things that are not yet present, but are inherent potentials in reality. It does not refer to illusion or to fantasy. This is the level of vision that spawns invention.

In the literature of human potential, this kind of vision often refers to seeing things that presently exist as human reality, but are not yet realities for that person. For example, speakers on human potential often encourage people to envision themselves as prosperous, or thin, or any other attribute they desire. This practice of envisioning desirable states is believed to help the person achieve them. It may be debatable whether or not this really works for most people, but the power of vision in guiding our lives is not debatable. In fact, such vision may be what most distinguishes us from the bum on the street who has lost the ability to see a desirable future, or any future at all for that matter.

The third level is what I call *pioneering vision*. It refers to the ability to *see desirable futures that are not there and that others do not believe can be there*. It involves breaking barriers or extending frontiers. It is about doing what others think impossible. It is the vision of breakthroughs. Pioneers are those who set out to break the limits of current human experience. They push the boundaries. They create new possibilities.

But this is not yet the full meaning of pioneering vision. It does not refer to the creation of oddities or odd behaviors, even if they have never been done before. It is not a vision of being in the *Guinness Book of World Records*. Pioneering vision refers to seeing the possibility of doing things that have not been done before, but that would be important to all of us if done. These visions are related to gains for human life, such as better health, expanded physical and mental abilities, access to the wonders of previously unknown realms, the rewards of new pleasures, greater satisfaction, fuller meaning, advancements in knowledge, unimagined abundance, or discoveries about the secrets of the universe. Pioneering visions are about extending the frontiers of the human experience.

There is one further test. Pioneering is not about doing things that are harmful or horrible, even though they have not been done before. It is not about following a Hitler, though his vision also had great power over human beings. On the contrary, to truly possess the power of vision we call pioneering, the vision must involve *seeing new possibilities that break through the limits of ordinary human experience in ways that are liberating and enlivening*. That is the attraction of the pioneering vision.

Let's test this definition against the visions of a few organizations that contributed to pioneering the world as we know it today.

PIONEERING VISIONS
THAT CHANGED OUR WORLD

Fords for All

Henry Ford's vision was to build a "motor car" everyone could afford. At that time, automobiles were expensive, beyond the price range of most people, and were being built by craftsmen in small quantities. It was not, however, a marketing problem. The American love for automobiles was born when local gentry in towns all over the country first drove those noisy horseless chariots down the dusty main streets of their towns. Perhaps Americans fell in love with them because the country was so large and so filled with "wide open" spaces. Or perhaps it was because of the egalitarian dream built into our democracy. Whatever the case, just as it is today, we covet new cars.

If Ford were to take advantage of this desire, however, if he were to achieve his vision, it would be necessary to sell large quantities of cars, thereby bringing down the cost per unit. This not only led Ford to pioneer a new design for automobiles, but to pioneer the assembly line and mass production processes as well. But Ford's vision went even further. He saw that people would be able to pack their friends and families into those cars, escape the crowded cities, and in a short time find themselves driving through some of the most beautiful country in the world. This further vision is a good example of the "liberating and enlivening" part of the definition for pioneering organizations described above. This part of the vision no doubt shaped the marketing of Model Ts, and it also gave an almost religious fervor to Ford's quest.

The Apple Revolution

Popular stories tell us that from the first, Steven Jobs saw the revolutionary nature of personal computers. He saw that personal computers could change not only the way people worked, but also the very way they thought. In one made-for-TV movie, Jobs is shown as dismissive of the demonstrations of the '60s, commenting that the demonstrators could not even imagine the real revolution that was coming. He was right. That vision was captured forcefully in the famous Super Bowl commercial described at the beginning of this chapter.

There is abundant testimony to the dedication and zeal of those early Apple employees. They literally felt they were on a Promethean quest, creating a new kind of "fire" to benefit the human race. The fact that established computing leaders believed there would be no demand for computers at home only spurred on the Apple employees. What did establishment types ever know, anyway? The Apple revolution would sweep those oppressive leaders and their organizations away, liberating the masses from the gray conformity of bureaucratic life. Not only did Jobs' vision change our lives then, but it is so robust that Apple is now leading a second pioneering transformation of personal computers.

Ritz-Carlton: The Standard for Service

Chip Bell, a leading consultant on customer service, frequently writes and speaks about Ritz-Carlton and its CEO, Horst Schultze. According to Chip, Mr. Schultze believes that an organization's vision should lift work endeavors to the level of a cause and that his job as CEO is to create a culture in which the employees experience their work as a calling. The Ritz-Carlton vision and culture not only inspired some of the highest levels of customer service in the world, but also pioneered the new wave of attention to customer service. The Ritz-Carlton credo precisely describes the company's commitment to the highest levels of service, and then goes further to envision the benefits to the customers: "The Ritz-Carlton experience enlivens the senses, instills well-being, and fulfills even the unexpressed wishes and needs of our guests."

The employees at Ritz-Carlton live the vision. This is typical of pioneering organizations, in which visions are not plaques on a wall, but articles of faith that guide and inspire everything employees do. One Ritz-Carlton basic says "any employee who receives a guest complaint 'owns' the complaint." They empower any employee to spend up to $2,000 to take care of an expressed customer need, and that is just a guideline, not an absolute limit.

My own personal experience of the hotel's service bears this out. When I was staying at the Ritz-Carlton in Tyson's Corner, Virginia, a few years back, I had to pull an all-nighter in preparation for a client's leadership retreat the next day. The maid who came in to turn back my bed listened to my tale of woe. A few minutes later, she returned with a fresh pot of strong coffee and some cookies. This continued on an hourly basis, and when she went off duty, another employee took up the watch. My work went much better, not just because of the coffee, but because of the caring. Working through the night was no longer such a lonely job.

Chip's favorite Ritz-Carlton story is from a woman who worked in one of the hotel's coffee shops in Naples, Florida. He asked her what she liked most about working there. He quotes her as saying that her work at Ritz-Carlton made her a better mother and wife. "I started doing things at home the same way I do them here," she said. "My husband and children noticed and after a time began to treat each other with the same kind of respect and courtesy. This completely changed our family life for the better." Pioneering visions not only change the world, but they stir the souls of the people who work with them and transform their lives.

The Federal Express

Fred Smith's vision in founding Federal Express was to be a jet age version of the Pony Express. Those are my words, not his, but they capture the spirit of his vision. He formed his company to meet a need the business world did not yet even know it had. As Ron Zemke, in his book *The Service Edge*, put it, the need was to "'absolutely, positively' get something—anything—somewhere overnight."[3] Many felt this was an unfeasible and unneeded service, so FedEx demonstrated its commitment and belief by guaranteeing it.

Fred Smith's vision, however, goes beyond the FedEx guarantee. It is a vision of exceptional service, of an organization and employees who do whatever it takes to deliver their cargo in perfect condition and on time every time. He regularly exhorts FedEx employees to remember why they are there, that they are not just delivering stuff. In their book *Managing Knock Your Socks Off Service*, Bell and Zemke report one of Smith's reminders to FedEx employees about the importance of their work. "We transport the most important cargo in the world," he said, "an organ for a vital transplant, a gift for a special ceremony, a factory part that may have halted a major enterprise."

The story of Jessica McClure, the little Texas girl trapped in a well several years ago, illustrates the degree to which Smith's vision has permeated his organization and given the world vital new possibilities that never existed before. The FedEx agent who received a late night request to provide transportation for drilling equipment needed in the rescue of the girl immediately dispatched a stand-by FedEx jet—without authorization and without knowing who would pay the bill. According to Ron Zemke, no one at FedEx finds that unusual.

The Nike Lifestyle

Simply put, Nike's operative vision was that a better running shoe would let people run further and faster and would encourage many more people to run. Its co-founder, coach Bill Bowerman, considered himself a teacher, but he was also an inventor and a visionary. His early design for an improved running shoe was based on a prototype molded in a waffle iron. This shoe and his earlier '60s book on jogging did a great deal to pioneer the popularity of running as a favored form of exercise. Literally millions turned off their TV sets, got up off their couches, and went out onto the paths, parks, and streets of the world—to run.

I remember when I first heeded this call and took up jogging in the late '70s, it was still something of a novelty to be running on some of the roads around Austin, Texas. Texans for a long time could not see how anyone would go anywhere in anything but a car or pickup. Men drove by as I ran, yelling colorful insults at me. And then Nike challenged us to "Just Do It." For a little over 20 years now, those same men who insulted me have been running. Today, Austin has more running trails in more beautiful places than any other city in the country, more runners per capita, and one of the largest annual road races. Nike got the world running. It launched a lifestyle that moved from running to natural foods, to a decline in smoking and drinking, to increased health and longevity for the human race. Bill Bowerman's vision was not really about a shoe; it was about a better life for all people of any age. And that was its power.

PIONEERING VISIONS COME IN MANY SIZES

Pioneering visions stir the soul. They open possibilities for us that did not exist before. They change our world for the better. Not all of them, however, have the scope and size of the famous examples just described. Each of those five impacted the whole world. Most pioneering visions are smaller. Some of them affect only one country, one region, or sometimes only one community. Some of them are relevant to only one industry or one segment of the population. They are nonetheless powerful and represent breakthroughs and new possibilities for those they touch.

The individuals who bring us these visions and those who work to achieve them can be just as inspired and just as motivated as the champions of large visions. And interestingly, many smaller ones set off chain reactions of pioneering changes that continue to grow until eventually they impact us all. In fact, the Nike story is itself an example of that kind of chain reaction.

Many of the examples to follow are small in scale and limited in scope, but they help us understand the range of such visions. Further, they illustrate the networked nature of the influence of such visions. Pioneering vision can be just as varied as the human race. A consideration of the full range helps bring them down from the high places of mythology to the reach of mere mortals like you and me. Pioneering possibilities exist everywhere. We have only to learn to see them. They are waiting for us. To illustrate this point, let's take a look at a few more pioneering visions.

Texas Instruments

In the early days at Texas Instruments the vision was of compression and speed through microcircuitry. Working that TI vision were the scientists of the Central Research Laboratories—many of whom were Iowa farm boys—who, in 1959, among other things, built the world's second working field emission microscope, allowing a few of us to be among the first human beings to see the emitted image of the silicone molecule. Unlocking the secrets of that molecule opened the new universe of possibilities known as the Information Age.

Southwest Airlines

Another vision of a different type is that of Herb Kelleher and the people at Southwest Airlines, who let my son, flying unaccompanied as a boy of nine, feel very grown-up by passing out peanuts to the other passengers. They were spreading love all over Texas. This happened more than once. My son considered himself part of the company. Southwest Airlines, with its lower fares and service to smaller cities made flight possible for many people who previously could not afford it or who had to drive long distances to get to a large city airport. This fundamentally changed the airline industry, but even more fundamentally altered our society. Families who were being scattered by the shifting of jobs and who were only infrequently able to see each other were now being brought closer together again. Grandma and Grandpa could now "move about the country" and play with their scattered grandchildren. Imagine our world if most had remained unable to fly.

Starbucks

Some visions are initially only about local markets, but the concepts embedded in them have such appeal to the public that they quickly spread. Howard Shultz's vision for Starbucks is one example. Initially, he thought that the popularity of espresso bars in Milan, Italy, might catch on in Seattle. That vision of providing an entire atmosphere for good coffee not only caught on in Seattle, but it quickly spread across the United States, setting a competitive standard that means we no longer have to drink dishwater coffee in most of the country's restaurants and airlines.

Whole Foods

In the food industry, Whole Foods Markets pioneered the natural food movement in this country, as well as total employee participation. The small staff in the company's first store was so dedicated that they pulled together and sandbagged their way through an Austin flood so they could reopen quickly and not deprive their customers of a healthy meal. Their vision was so compelling that Whole Foods Markets has spread across the country.

Kinko's

The Kinko's story has interesting parallels. Beginning in a small space in a hamburger stand near the University of California at Santa Barbara, Kinko's is now one of the "musts" for neighborhoods that would attract entrepreneurs and young professionals. My own experience is a good example. Three years ago, I sold my expensive, large-volume copy machine. The convenience of having it in my home office did not even compare with the high-speed equipment at Kinko's. Also, the staff there continues to take an interest in my business and regularly performs miracles when I most need them.

The Arts and Entertainment

A small but beautiful vision is KMFA, perhaps the nation's only 24-hour, listener-supported, classical radio station, which has been on the air in Austin, Texas, for the past 33 years. Before that, there was KMFA's predecessor, the first exclusively FM commercial radio station in Texas, and Rod Kennedy, whose vision pioneered both stations, as well as the Kerrville Folk Festival. These visions led to the popular PBS program *Austin City Limits*, which brought many of the performers from the festival, and other well-known performers like Willie Nelson and Michael Martin Murphy, into living rooms across the nation. It created a wave of popularity as folk-country became hip.

IC² & the Global Economy

The vision/mission of IC² has all the ingredients of pioneering visions and their impacts on our world. They see their vision as "a quest for constructive forms of capitalism that will allow communities and nations to grow and prosper." Their mission is "to combine technology, entrepreneurship, and education to improve the world via wealth creation and prosperity sharing." This vision led to their playing a catalytic role in the extraordinary growth of high-tech businesses in Austin. They are now spreading the knowledge gained from their success there to the rest of the world through their "technopolis" building program and services. This may contribute to the needed breakthrough to eliminate not only the digital divide around the world, but to eliminate the suffering that comes from extreme poverty and poor education.

Human Services

Years ago, in the field of human services, a man named Jules Sugerman not only pioneered the Head Start program, but passionately defended and preserved it from the ax of its critics. And there are people like Max Arrell, Jimmy Jackson, and Tom Word at the Texas Rehabilitation Commission and their pioneering visions for full participation of people with disabilities. Those visions helped catalyze the Americans with Disabilities Act and a world of new possibilities through accessibility. On another front, community schools all across the country owe a debt to the pioneering vision of Patricia Otis Stephens, who saw that people in the community could create their own schools, bringing together the resources of hundreds of previously fragmented agency efforts. An earlier vision that influenced all of these was that of Lyndon Johnson with his commitment to civil rights and his Texas determination to help the poor. And the vision of his teacher, Sam Rayburn, whose "little school room" was a place where several presidents, both Republican and Democrat, came to learn the practical reality that is the genius of the American political process

There are thousands of such stories worth telling. Visions like these ennoble human life.

THE DEGRADATION OF VISION

The importance of vision must not be underestimated. The potential trivialization of vision is one of the dangers resulting from a decline in individualism. Vision is a unique capacity of the human mind—the ability to see better possibilities. To review, it is a remarkable capacity, in that it means that people are able to see things that *do not yet exist*! Vision can be shared, and someone else's vision can stimulate mine, but vision is something that happens initially in the individual human mind. Everyone has the capacity. In some it is developed more than in others. In individualists, it is developed to its highest potential, due to their willingness to break from the fetters of conventional wisdom. When individualism is suppressed, vision will still occur, but it may be about adjustments rather than breakthroughs. Pioneering vision is the province of individualism. (Chapter 4 explores this more fully.)

In the last 15 years, a great deal of time, attention, and money have gone into activities designed to evoke vision. Some of this resulted only in silly, formal statements hanging on corporate walls, but much of it resulted in the intense exploration of desirable possibilities. But even for companies that have taken vision seriously, problems can arise. And in the trenches, there will never be clear signs that a degradation of vision has occurred. Leaders must be aware that certain practices have the potential to actually discourage the deep inquiries of individualists, thus cheapening vision. Here are a few to watch for:

* The Vision Fad: If we are not careful, the valuable vision work going on in today's organizations will become too commonplace. People will see it as nothing more than an exercise. There is already a fair amount of cynicism surrounding such activities.

* Brainstormed Blindness: Brainstorming is becoming an exercise in facile cleverness. The storming has gone out of it. We may need to encourage more intense struggles to imagine and to understand. Independent thought often delves deeper.

* Incremental Improvement: Are we incrementally improving employees into small thinking, rather than bold ideas?

* Super Vision: When vision from the top dominates, others may think it is not important for them to try to see new possibilities. In this highly competitive knowledge age, it is important for many to envision pioneering possibilities and to show the courage of their convictions in advocating them.

* E-llusion: There is so much excitement about every new invention related to IT and the Internet that one might wonder if *Vision* is the latest video game. Very soon, it will take more than added features, speed, and connection to be a pioneer. Dependability is needed. In addition to more information, what about greater learning, deeper understanding, and more time? Will the Internet be overwhelmed with commerce, entertainment, hate groups, hackers, and rapid misinformation, or will it achieve long-needed breakthroughs in building trust, global understanding, universal education, an end to hunger,

total health care, and world peace. Pioneering vision is needed in advancing technology most of all.

WE NEED PIONEERING VISIONS FROM EVERYONE

Up to this point in history, pioneering has been only for the few. The many were needed to tend the home fires. It took masses of people doing the same things to serve the needs of the human race.

This is no longer the case. Machines are taking over the jobs of mass production. Increasingly, the new jobs call for custom solutions. This does not only create new opportunities for vision, it creates demand. After thousands of years of preparation, the universe is calling forth the amazing reservoirs of vision that lay latent in the human race. Pioneering vision is needed from all.

Breakthroughs are needed in every profession and every craft. Breakthroughs are needed to solve the problems of the world. Breakthroughs are needed in every industry. Some industries are stagnating, and we are suffering from their lack of innovation. How long has it been since there were any improvements in commercial passenger aircraft, for instance? Finding ways to crowd in more seats is not pioneering. Thank you, American Airlines for your recent industry-changing initiative to give passengers more leg room again. We need more pioneering of this sort from the airlines and from the aircraft manufacturers as well. When was the last time there were any great gains in highway design and road construction? And how long will we have to wait for sources of energy that can abundantly support the human race without destroying our planet and our only home?

Breakthroughs are needed in every organization, every department, every system, every job. Breakthroughs are the first item on the job descriptions for most jobs in the 21st century. If you are a leader, breakthroughs are your business. More bells and whistles will not meet the need.

STIMULATING VISION
AND PREVENTING ITS DEGRADATION

Here are a few ways leaders can stimulate pioneering visions in their organizations and prevent the degradation of the company's vision:

1. Provide a means for each employee to experience the organization's products or services *as the customer experiences them*. Not only will employees begin to see ways to improve what your organization offers, but they will also begin to "feel" the importance of the contribution they can make.

2. Have your employees write down their ideas about better products and services, and also their ideas about ways to improve the work they do in their units.

3. Work with employees to understand the barriers to improvement in the way of breakthroughs.

4. Have employees visualize the breakthrough point, talk about what they see, and plan ways to get there.

5. Organize the pioneering mission and make it a matter of urgency.

This list is by no means exhaustive, but it can help you think about how to not only improve, but to pioneer. For more help with action steps, see Part 2 of this book.

THE MESSAGE

The message of this chapter is that it is possible to call forth the capacity for pioneering vision in men and women in organizations all over the world. In every industry—from dry-cleaning and home-building to aerospace and cyberspace—in every organization, in every department, in every team, and in every job. It is badly needed.

It is also what moves an organization beyond peak performance to the extraordinary performance of pioneering. It is good for business, and it is good for the world. And it is there for the taking—pioneering vision in abundance just beneath the surface of socially induced sleep, waiting in the souls of most women and men, yearning to be called into service for the needs of our time. You have only to ask.

From Conflict
to Convergence 3

*T*he very nature of organizations requires a convergence of resources and effort. Yet organizations are continually plagued by conflicting interests. Today's technology-driven organizations are no exception. For them to succeed, everything must flow together seamlessly. Leaders are charged with making that happen. Leaders must keep in mind that the shifting nature of work and the accelerating expectations of the marketplace bring with them a highly charged package of divergent and competing interests. The potential for conflicting agendas is high.

Given the onrush of new technologies, most new jobs today not only require thinking, but independent thinking at that. We have developed an unprecedented need for individualists. (Individual self-interests are important motivators for all people, but individualists are more openly insistent about getting theirs met.) The increased complexity of work and systems, however, means that these jobs also call for the highest levels of teamwork in history. And as we know, there has always been a tension between teamwork and individualism. Today, when that tension causes even a small decline in performance, the results to companies can be devastating.

The problem is compounded by the digital divide and the differing needs of a minority who still perform poorly paid manual labor that offers little opportunity for intellectual input and little opportunity for the development of capacities that will prepare them for better jobs. At the same time, there is a growing shortage of qualified people available for the higher-paying "knowledge" jobs. All of this is exacerbated by the accelerating expectations of investors for record returns on their investment. The potential clash of interests in these post-industrial organizations is monumental, and it comes at a time when change and global competition demand the highest levels of commitment and performance ever seen. This is the challenge for leadership in our time. The 21st century will belong to those organizations that seek and find a true convergence of these competing interests.

This is all made more difficult given the deep roots and psychological scars of this fundamental organizational conflict. The history of organizations, indeed the history of the human race, has been a story of conflict resulting from the interests of some overpowering the interests of others. The main players in the epic power struggle have always taken the parts of leaders, organized groups, and strong individualists. Leaders have concerned themselves with deciding which human beings would be rewarded and which ones would be discarded, as well as what each would be paid and for what type of labor. The organized groups within society either supported the leaders or banded around strong individualists to oppose them. When they succeeded, these rebel individualists frequently became obsessed with wealth and power rather than using the opportunity to serve the community; they betrayed the groups that supported them in overthrowing the previous leaders. And so the story goes.

The human species has experimented with many different arrangements of these three protagonists. Our sympathies and support tends to shift according to the role we currently fill and our own personal interests, whether we acknowledge them or not. But we must resolve to end the drama by moving from conflict to convergence. The economic realities of our time will give us no other choice.

When organizational practices produce a true convergence of interests, the results are so extraordinary that we have trouble believing them, even when we take part in making them happen. Consequently, we typically forget and resume our old roles and our old ways. Convergence, of course, is achieved by degrees, and there are corresponding degrees of heightened performance. Convergence sometimes results from relatively simple organizational development practices and affects only a portion of an organization. At other times, all of an organization's practices may culminate in a convergence so complete that the entire organization is rocketed ahead. Here are a few recent examples of highly successful convergent efforts to help us remember the positive results.

At Abbott Labs a few years ago, a cross-functional group achieved a convergence that served all units involved, satisfied the outspoken individualists, and gained the support of the management. The almost instantaneous result was a 63 percent gain in the production of zero-defect intraveneous (IV) bags. At ITT, a director of human resources who facilitated such an effort reported a gain of over 300 percent in the speed of connecting their customers. At the Texas Rehabilitation Commission, it was an increase ranging from 27 to 60 percent in the number of clients whose rehabilitation resulted in employment. And at the Vignette Corporation, in the first year after the company's IPO, the value of stock rose by over 1,000 percent, and its long-range performance looks promising since Vignette is making significant gains toward profitability. Most of us know of such stories. The argument here is for developing organizations in which these practices become the norm.

DIVERGENT INTERESTS

A brief analysis of the divergent interests and purposes of individualism, teamwork, and leadership will demonstrate the challenge of finding a convergence. It will also reveal some potential avenues for convergence.

Individualism

Individualism is frequently seen as threatening to the interests of others. Furthermore, strong individualists are often accused of serving self-interests only, and sometimes they are guilty. But at its best, individualism also involves seeing and championing a better way of doing things that benefits others as well. From this came the notion of "enlightened self-interest."

Healthy individualism focuses first on shouldering the responsibility for taking care of self and family. This is the essence of self-reliance and the antidote to helplessness and dependency. It does not, however, stop there—it never has. Healthy individualists also want to make a valued contribution; that is part of paying their own way. Organizational studies and surveys have consistently shown that most people, including individualists, want to do a good job.

Individualists are also intensely interested in having and exercising freedom of thought, choice, and action. They demand participation and involvement, but they often become frustrated by the slowness and sluggishness of some of the team activities they are asked to participate in today. There is also a growing feeling that many teams suppress divergent individual opinions.

Individualists want to continue to grow and learn new things, and they seek jobs that let them do so. Individualists are constantly looking for better ways to do things—vision is their natural state. They also love to win, but healthy individualists do not have to do so at the expense of others. Their drive is to meet the challenge and to do their personal best. Under certain toxic family or cultural conditions, these natural motivations can become perverted, resulting in an obsession to get more stuff and to conquer others.

Teamwork

The initial impetus for teamwork is to look for increased effectiveness—to gain advantage from the strength of numbers or to seek synergies. It is focused on getting and giving help to do what needs to be done. Since human beings are naturally social animals, teamwork additionally has the purpose of providing a sense of belonging and the comfort that comes from community. Furthermore, there is nothing quite like the spirit and exhilaration of being on a winning team.

Teamwork is focused on the task: getting the job done. However, when teamwork becomes institutionalized into teams, new purpose and new dynamics enter. Teams are the domain of group dynamics. As a result of their affiliation purposes, teams value loyalty and seek to protect the group. This can result in a challenge to leadership and the suppression of individualism. By extension, groups and teams are often invested in preserving traditions, and frequently they are the source of resistance to change. When strong groups or teams perceive a threat to their members or to the existence of the group, they can be fiercely protective. They can also take on the aggressive psychology and behavior of gangs and lynch mobs.

Leadership

Leadership is intended to bring people together to achieve certain purposes. It is the genesis of organization, the guardian of its resources, and the embodiment of its authority. Its legitimate aim is the well-being of the organization and the accomplishment of the organization's purposes. In corporate life, that includes reaching sales and revenue goals, maintaining market share, recruiting and retaining productive employees, satisfying customers, and making a profit for investors. Leadership pursues the goals of the organization by focusing attention and resources on current performance, while at the same time seeking future opportunities. At its best, leadership earns the respect of employees and inspires them to peak performance.

Leadership is in a position to encourage or suppress both individualism and teamwork. It can encourage one while suppressing the other, play one against the other, decide what kind of contribution is required from each, and decide how to value and reward each. It can see the individuals and work groups that comprise the organization as expendable resources to be exploited for the benefit of the organization and its leaders. Or leadership can value and support individuals and work groups as entities with inalienable rights, whose partnership is vital. It can seek a convergence of interests that will benefit all. Too frequently, however, leadership becomes obsessed with serving its own interests and with preserving its power. In the process, it often targets individualists as potential enemies and creates conflict within and between teams.

To summarize, given their divergent interests, teamwork and individualism can clash over what and how things should be done, pull in opposite directions, or provide an engine of creative tension that can rocket an organization toward its vision. Frequently, groups or teams play an important role as the guardians of continuity, while individuals serve as the arrows of change. When they combine forces and align with leadership, highly beneficial results are possible. When they do not, resistance and even revolution are the result.

THREE KINDS OF CONTRIBUTION

The interplay of these divergent interests becomes even more complex when we consider that three different kinds of effort and three different kinds of contribution are possible—physical, intellectual, and emotional. Emotional contribution refers to enthusiasm, energy, and spirit; physical contribution refers to muscular effort, skills, resources, and capital; and intellectual contribution refers to knowledge, ideas, innovations, and breakthroughs.

All or any one of these potential contributions can be *made, encouraged, supported, resisted,* or *suppressed* by all or any one of the three entities of leadership, teamwork, or individualism. For example, leaders may encourage physical contributions from both teams and individuals, but suppress intellectual contributions. This was the case for most of human history. In recent years, leaders have encouraged the ideas of teams, while teams are frequently critical of the ideas of some of their most outspoken individualists. Leaders often want people to leave their *personal* emotions at home, but are vitally concerned about the *workplace* emotions they call spirit or morale. Teams often want less talk (intellectual) and more action (physical) out of their individual members. Individualists are often skeptical of ideas generated by a committee.

THREE PRINCIPLES FOR CONVERGENCE

Given the maze of purposes described above, surprisingly only three principles are needed to bring them into alignment. The essence of these three principles were embedded in early democratic thought. They are also the core dynamic in the formation of pioneering organizations.

1. Individuals are the fundamental units of organization. They are not tools of production. They are conscious beings who exercise personal choice. Each individual counts. In today's world, individualism is indispensable. There are always *legitimate* differences in self-interests, opinions, and beliefs. Differences are valuable. They serve as raw material that fuels the organization's engine. The vision here is of a new birth of individualism that understands its interdependence.

2. Teamwork is the essence of organization. It is not just a desirable behavior. We all need help from others. No individual is completely independent, and today all jobs are interconnected. Teamwork at its best is aligned individualism. The vision here is of teamwork free from peer oppression and provincial protectionism.

3. Leadership is the galvanizing vision and energy of organization. It brings people together in service of the common enterprise. The legitimate aim of leadership (authority) is the well-being of the whole. The organization as a whole is a conscious system that exists as its constituent parts within an ecology of interdependent exchange. The vision here is of leadership that sees the whole of the organization in each employee and in every team as they work together to serve the needs of their customers, communities, and the world. Leadership is the art of understanding the needs and interests of all involved and of finding a convergence of interests that propels the performance of the organization.

APPLYING THE PRINCIPLES OF CONVERGENCE

While these principles are simple, their application is not. Divinity is in the details. The next three chapters will examine their application in depth. For now, let's briefly consider some current organizational conditions that will help and hinder in developing the kinds of individualism, teamwork, and leadership described above.

For Individualism

Individualism does not occur in isolation; it is defined by the context of community. This has always been true, but it is especially true in today's organizations. Individualists need to interact with a community of minds to differentiate and sharpen their ideas. They need community as a lab for their visions. Thoreau's thinking did not begin at Walden Pond. This characteristic of individualism can greatly assist in the development of convergent, pioneering organizations, provided that individualistic thinking and the debate of ideas is welcomed and honored rather than suppressed. It also helps when today's transient organizations find ways to reinvent community.

One problem individualism has in organizations today is that independent thought has been overwhelmed by a glut of glib information and the overuse of group techniques like brainstorming. Far too much of the team training has also resulted in "group-think" even though that was certainly not anyone's intention. The powerful effects of peer pressure were simply not sufficiently anticipated. Organizations need to provide many opportunities for individual reflection and the expression of ideas. It does not have to be time consuming, but it needs to happen frequently. The next chapter will discuss numerous ways to do this simply and cheaply.

Beyond reflection, it is important that organizations encourage a lively debate of opinions. Too many forms of personality and communication training have overemphasized "nice." Some of the most productive debates can get quite raucous before reaching resolution. The direction should be in developing independent thinking and individuals who stand up for their convictions but allow others to do so as well. Too much concern about not causing offense can weaken everyone. Political correctness has compounded the problem. Strong individualists are able to move past arguments once they are worked through to resolution. They are able to then join those they have disagreed with in developing powerful plans and in committing to them totally. This produces results that are extraordinarily superior to the plans that come from "nice," politically correct, team play.

For Teamwork

What is needed most is teamwork in all directions rather than a strong bonding into teams. Such bonding often results in protective and aggressive behaviors toward others rather than teamwork. In my practice, the strongest examples of teamwork I have seen take the form of aligned individualism, not peer bonding. As I said above, individualists, intent on getting something done, will commit totally to a plan of action once it is agreed to. That is often after intense debate about the actions to be taken—not personal sharing.

The behaviors for this kind of teamwork are not what has been called for in so many training sessions on teams. The needed behaviors are not about understanding our personality or cultural differences. They are about surfacing and resolving differences of opinion about the work to be done. When people focus fully on what to do or how best to do it together, they tend to go blind to personal differences as something to be concerned about. They stop generalizing. When each person focuses on doing his or her part, personal differences become a resource for getting the job done. Furthermore, teamwork behaviors are also not primarily about being sensitive to and nurturing others in the group. Of course, it is important to comfort and support each other in times of adversity, either at home or on the job. But the main attention goes to helping each other do what is needed to get the job done and to reach agreed-upon goals. It is about work. This kind of teamwork maintains an awareness of the group as a whole and why it exists. It values individuals and the contributions they can make to the common effort. It supports individuals and helps them solve problems that are hindering them in getting the job done, whether those problems are work-related or personal. But it is still focused on the job to be done, rather than making sympathy, nurturing, and comfort its main business.

For Leadership

Most leaders today employ some degree of participative management. Twenty years ago that was not the case. As a result, they are more in touch with employees and in a better position to work toward a convergence of interests. Also, a very high percentage of leaders have seen some powerful positive results come from involving employees in many of the organization's strategy and planning activities. In spite of these results, however, they are still bound to many old, control-centered management practices. They are stuck in old paradigms and old beliefs, often reinforced by big consulting firms and far too many business school courses. Their beliefs and therefore their practices have not caught up with their eyes and their own direct experience. Consequently, most of them have not yet seen that they can design everything around a highly participative, convergent approach.

Marketplace forces, however, are moving leaders in the right direction. In the last half century, as work transformed from procuring and processing raw material to producing ever more complex and compressed technological devices, the need for a radical shift— toward encouraging the contribution of ideas from *both* teams and individuals—became apparent. In practice, this shift has been incomplete, however, due to both the negative press given to individual self-interest and the failure to tangibly reward teamwork. With this shift of emphasis from physical work (which is visible) to innovative ideas and commitment (which are invisible), the factor of individual choice in deciding to contribute or withhold effort and ideas has become paramount.

That choice is made within each individual employee; managers can encourage people to give their best effort, but beyond the obvious, they can only guess at the choice being made. They cannot "manage" it. Their best bet is to become skillful in leading processes that involve employees in making organizational decisions. If done with openness and sincerity, these processes will ultimately surface hidden interests and concerns and move toward a convergence of interests. This is not yet happening on a constant enough basis, but there are signs of a growing awareness that something like this is needed. One sign of this is the tremendous increase in the use of employee surveys. Another sign is that many managers today are concerned with the difference between *compliance* and *commitment* in their impact on the added innovation and emotional energy released for reaching goals. They have realized that the extra energy that comes from commitment (an emotion) is a differentiating characteristic of many winning companies. The examples at Starbucks, Vignette, and the Post Ranch Inn of creative compensation and benefit packages, and of extensive collaboration with employees on just about everything are evidence of the power of convergent practices.

THE CONVERGENT-DEMOCRATIC LEADERSHIP ARCHETYPE

Over the course of human history, a variety of organizational forms emerged as attempted solutions to the power struggle between leaders, groups, and individualists. Six organizational archetypes can be identified: authoritarian, aristocratic, collectivist, dictatorship, self-regulating/laissez-faire, and convergent-democratic. These archetypes represent different distributions of power favoring one of the entities over the others or creating alliances between two of them. Only the convergent-democratic seeks a convergence of the interests of all three. Each of these forms also has its own characteristic pattern of encouraging or discouraging physical, intellectual, or emotional inputs; the convergent-democratic is the most successful.

In the convergent-democratic archetype, leadership pursues the legitimate aim of serving the well-being of the whole by honoring, encouraging, empowering, aligning, and integrating the interests of both individualism and teamwork and their respective contributions toward the achievement of private, reciprocal, and mutual aims. Such organizations seek a convergence of interests. When the organization is a government, as is the case with all the industrial democracies, it encourages and attempts to integrate the needs and contributions of entrepreneurs and environmentalists, developers and neighborhoods, backpackers and open-range ranchers.

The strength of such organizations, with their protection of individual freedom and choice, is that they inspire the fullest possible range of committed human contribution. The weakness comes with the weakening social ties of industrial and post-industrial society, in which there is a loss of appreciation for the importance of the common good. Individual selfishness and special-interest groups can then overwhelm the natural desire to also serve community.

The dominant world view of this organizational archetype is that opportunity abounds, that the possible gains are worth the risks, that change creates new opportunities, and that more resources are always obtainable—or if they are not, they can be invented. That can blind democratic organizations to the dangers they themselves create by damage to and depletion of natural resources. Many believe we have depleted the earth's resources and contaminated it to the point that we are in mortal danger and that the changes we have put in motion can only lead to loss. They may be right.

I would argue, however, that the stage is set, that the conditions of necessity and opportunity have reached a critical mass, and that we are on the threshold of an unprecedented age of pioneering. To fulfill this possibility, we must risk moving past our paralyzed state of polarized political and economic polemics in an effort to gain all that is needed for a golden age that benefits all mankind. Nothing short of a convergence of interests will get us there.

TODAY'S CONVERGENT ORGANIZATIONS

Let's consider a few organizations that achieved, at least at points, such a convergence by applying pioneering principles.

The Vignette Corporation is one of the most complete examples of a convergence that I have seen. They intentionally designed it that way. Other examples described in Part III are Starbucks, The Post Ranch Inn, and the convergence catalyzing organization, IC². At

Vignette, two ideas guided their design: to create an organization that was (1) market driven, not product driven, and (2) was an adult environment. The first idea led them to seek ways to make the Web work better for their client companies, not try to dazzle them with technological wizardry. As a result, they have the software that runs five of the top Web sites in the United States.

The second idea led them to place the balance of power in the company with teams and with individuals. Also, every single person who joins the company is given stock. This is a common feature in most of the IT companies in the Austin area. It has produced a significant population of young rich people who are now finding opportunities to give something back to the community. A few critics have complained that the IT companies expect unlimited hours in return for this stock and that this is a new form of worker exploitation. Most of these wealthy young employees, however, see the hours as the honorable heritage of America's entrepreneurs and small business owners.

Another striking example of convergence is found in a story that Fred Reicheld tells, in his book, *The Loyalty Effect*.[4] It is an example of how State Farm provided extraordinary customer service that converged with the company's financial interests. In the aftermath of Hurricane Andrew in 1992 which produced unusually large claims, many insurance companies, in an attempt to keep losses under control, covered the claims required by their contracts, then refused to renew customer policies to avoid future losses. State Farm, on the other hand, *paid more than their policies required* to bring some previously substandard roofs up to code. They saw this as a good way to reward customer loyalty and secure it in the future. But more interestingly, according to State Farm's general counsel at the time, C. A. Ingham, they saw it as a way to prevent damage in the future to houses that they intended to be insuring. State Farm expects its customers to stay with the company for years, so this approach saves everyone money in the long run.

Another exceptional example of the power of convergence occurred in 1991 in one of the area offices of The Texas

Rehabilitation Commission in the Rio Grande Valley. A recent federal policy had severely limited funds that could be spent addressing some non-severe forms of disability that resulted from the stoop labor work of the migrant farm workers there. This was the most common need in the Rio Grande Valley and not only limited the income of many families, but depressed the economy of the region. Not providing help also caused the employees of the center to lose the respect and regard of their friends, relatives, and neighbors in the tight-knit Mexican-American community of the Valley. This further resulted in a depressed and nonproductive center staff.

In an off-site planning session devoted to finding a solution for this problem, the staff created a number of strategies that were within the guidelines to mobilize local resources and coordinate the funds available from several other agencies. The staff also devised ways to maximize the impact of their own efforts and the funds that they could spend. One result was that TRC led a community-wide effort that addressed most of the non-severe stoop-labor injuries and increased the income of local families. A more striking result, however, was that the center's employees were so committed to their plan, and the way that it served everyone's interests, that they achieved a sixty-percent increase in successful employment for their rehabilitation clients. In one year, they moved from being the poorest performing office in TRC to being its top performer. Convergence works!

THE CONVERGENT POWER OF PIONEERING

Pioneering is a powerful force for creating a convergence of interests. It brings people together in a mutual quest to satisfy a pressing need or to create new possibilities for their organizations and for the human race. It calls forth the highest levels of both individualism and teamwork. Organizations whose aims are only about maximizing profits or satisfying special interest groups will not benefit from this exceptional power. They will have to work hard to achieve convergence. Only those pioneering organizations that answer the call to move forward, finding a way toward a better day for us all, can fully know the joys and rewards of such a mutuality of purpose.

Interdependent
Individualism 4

My introduction to the concept of individualism came when I was 15. I was a good kid in a small town, a Boy Scout, a good student; I performed community service and was always courteous to adults. I guess that was why it surprised my typing teacher, Mrs. Frost, who was also the entire business faculty, when I protested over the cold room in which we had to somehow loosen our fingers for typing. When she refused to do anything about it, I circulated a petition through all of the typing classes, getting about 80 percent of the other students to sign it. As she had the heat turned up, she said she had not realized I was a "rugged individualist." I did not know exactly what that term meant, and I was not sure it was good, but from that point on she took a real liking to me. And I became fascinated by the idea of individualism.

UNDERSTANDING INDIVIDUALISM

There has always been an uneasy relationship between society and individualism. Individualists don't conform. They critique and challenge the social order. They often push for change. Frequently, they are abrasive, and sometimes they pose a threat to established authority. This makes other people uncomfortable. Still, individualism is tolerated and even valued as long as it does not become

69

excessively self-serving or destructive. When that occurs, such deviant individualists are either thrown in jail or buy impunity with payoffs to law enforcement officers or bribes to politicians. This has been true throughout history. But haven't our historical heroes typically been individualists? What then accounts for the ascendance of individualism to a cultural ideal? How did our heroes' individualism emerge as a positive force that people valued?

Let's review. The Golden Age of Individualism began with the Renaissance, emerging in the form of an exploration of the heavens and discoveries on the seas. It found expression in colonial America, grew in popularity with the writings of Rousseau in early 18th century France, became a force in the American and French Revolutions, reached maturity in the Constitution of the United States, expanded with the advancing frontier, and served as a philosophical foundation for the growth of enterprise in the West throughout the 19th century. Since approximately 1929 it has been in decline.

In the 500 years of its golden age, individualism emerged from a seemingly set, stable, and secure social context, stirred things up, and flourished as a result of two simultaneous conditions. One condition was the barely conscious but widespread *increase of doubt* about the social order, its institutions, and its version of truth. The other was an *accumulation of new perspectives and possibilities* that had been slowly building for a long time, but that had gone largely unnoticed. When both of these factors—one pushing, the other pulling—converge in a conscious awareness that conventional wisdom may not be right, conditions are fertile for the rise of individualism.[5]

In that cultural uncertainty, a few "individualists" are drawn to understand how things truly are and to envision how they might be made better. They have the sense that it is up to them, that there is both the necessity and the opportunity to reach a new understanding and to take action on it. As they struggle to deal with this unsettling new reality, their thoughts and actions stimulate still more doubt about the social order, and their discoveries lead to even greater perspective shifts. It is this kind of individualism our society thrives on and encourages—even needs.

From the past, then, we learn two basic principles. First, individualism is both born of and pioneers new ages. And second, a scarcity of individualism leads to stagnation and social decline.

What then are the common elements in diverse social settings that develop and nurture a set of psychological strengths we call individualism? By pinpointing common conditions, we have the initial ingredients for effecting the return of individualism to meet the challenges of our time.

Let's consider the defining characteristics of individualism. Traditionally, individualism meant independence of thought, the courage of one's convictions, and a high degree of self-reliance. I would argue that individualism has also always been characterized by a strong sense of community and the desire to make a contribution. I see five conditions that are required for individualism to emerge. They can be thought of as the *psychological supports* necessary for developing the *psychological strengths* found in individualism.

Development Requires 5 Psychological Supports	Results in 5 Psychological Strengths
1. Strong social ties	1. A sense of belonging
2. Encouragement to think for self	2. Inquiring, independent mind
3. Support for self-direction	3. Courage of convictions
4. Freedom of action	4. Self-reliance
5. Opportunity to contribute	5. Self-esteem from service

If the conditions needed for positive individualism are so apparent, why then has organizational individualism been on the decline for the last two-thirds of the century? Let's consider this in depth.

DETRIMENTAL SOCIAL FORCES

A Crowd of Strangers:
Weakened Social Ties—Loss of Sense of Belonging

Since the late 1920s, a steadily increasing stream of people has moved from rural and small town roots to the cities in search of work. In doing so, they left the familiarity of lifetime friends and extended families. They found themselves surrounded by people they did not know, and they felt anxiety in not knowing how this crowd of strangers might react. Rather than using the freedom of greater anonymity to express more of their individuality, most of them became more cautious, kept their opinions to themselves, and tried to fit in. They lost their sense of belonging. As we shall see below, the downsizing fad of the last decade has compounded that loss.

In more recent times, people who grow up in the inner cities with networks of friends and ties to the daily lives of their neighborhoods experience the same uprooting as they follow job opportunities to the suburbs. Unfortunately, most never get the education needed to have that possibility. Too often, the sense of belonging in the inner-city neighborhoods is overwhelmed by poverty, resulting in an insecure banding into gangs and the sacrifice of individuality.

In both cases of migration, of course, if these "industrial immigrants" stay put for a while, their children form ties in the new environment and again experience a sense of belonging that could nurture individuality. Given other forces, however, these potential individualists are often overwhelmed by the pressure to fit in as a means to success.

The Fast Lane:
No Time to Think—Decline in Independent Thinking

In the move to the cities, not only did people lose social ties, they also lost time. Everything speeded up. The rhythms of rural life were replaced by the rush of city life. There never seemed to be enough time to get it all done. There was no "quittin' time." The time for reflection, the time to think things through and to form one's own opinions, dwindled. And worse, given the pressures of their jobs, parents found less time to listen to their kids—to listen to the novel theories and fanciful ideas. These are the origins of independent thought and inquiring minds, and they must be encouraged and nurtured. Most parents, even conscientious ones, barely have time to see to it that their children do their homework. Sadly, given standardized testing, there is little room for independent thought in homework these days.

Keeping Up Appearances and Peer-Referencing: Loss of Independent Thought and Will To Be Different

There has always been a certain amount of pressure to conform, and early editions of the Sears & Roebuck catalogue may have spurred an impulse to keep up with the Joneses. But since the advent of radio, the accelerating power of mass advertising has overwhelmed the innate desire to be oneself. From an early age, we are so saturated with images of what it means to be successful human beings that we gain little ability to form our own ideas about it. To be sure, we always imitated, but at least we had some choice of adult models. Today, we can still pick our heroes, but our lack of contact with adults in the community and the dominance of the media have largely limited our choices to sports, movies, or music. Within those confines, we can be different. We can choose to dress differently, for example, but the choice to be "alternative" is also a fad—another peer-referenced way to fit in.

This is not just a matter of dress, of appearance, or of costuming. Yes, it is still possible to do what is necessary to keep up appearances and still maintain a healthy independence of thought. But that is made increasingly difficult by fad language. It is not only important to dress right, but you must also say the right things. Language is the foundation of thought.

Finally, mass culture has made it mandatory to join. You may be in the "in" group or the "out" group, but either way you are in a group. Peer-referencing has become dominant in our time. Against these odds, it takes a lot of courage to go your own way.

Hired Hands and Job Insecurity:
Loss of Self-direction, Declining Self-reliance and Courage of Convictions

In *The Grapes of Wrath*, John Steinbeck captured the helplessness that came with a loss of self-reliance. True, the hero emerged as a strong individualist, but that's fiction. In real life, individualism has been in decline since the severe droughts and the Great Depression of the 1930s. Those dislocations ushered in the "Age of the Hired Hand." People learned it was a good idea to keep their opinions to themselves if they wanted to keep their jobs. Individualism suffered. In spite of widespread employee involvement in the last 15 years, many people still hold this belief.

Overruled:
Restricted Movement and Diminished Self-reliance

There was a time when children could roam, explore, adventure— when they could try out their wings without adult supervision. There was a time when it was safe. But over the last 30 years children have increasingly found their movements scrutinized. I watched as increasingly my children were supervised on the playgrounds, as adults began to organize their play for them, and as finally they were even lined up to march to the school lunchroom. I have seen teenagers in juvenile detention for things that would have gotten us a talking-to when I was growing up. There are a great many more rules, and a great many more laws and lawsuits. Our perceived need to provide protection and safety may be costing our children a loss of self-reliance.

Not Counted On:
Less Opportunity to Contribute—Exiled Self-esteem

There has been increasing, and controversial, attention in recent years to the need for developing self-esteem. It has spawned an array of new programs in schools and sold a forest of self-help books. If self-esteem could be self-induced, we would probably be witnessing a tremendous growth in individualism. Unfortunately, this is not the case. Self-esteem is based on service, not on self-talk. It is based on being able to make a contribution, to help, to be counted on. Just beyond the "I can do that myself!" assertion of two-year-olds is the request to "Let me help." When adults let them help, recognize their efforts, and finally, count on their contributions, self-esteem is born.

Given our modern appliances, busy schedules, and a wrong idea of childhood, we have stopped giving children the opportunity to contribute and make a difference. They are simply supposed to enjoy their childhood and do their schoolwork. They have no real role in life. It is postponed. In a real sense, they have become exiles, left to develop their own culture and to depend on peer-acceptance as the only measure of self-worth. No wonder some of them have become murderers and many more have become suicidal. It is not enough for adults to participate in their activities; they must be allowed to participate in ours. They must be allowed to contribute and make a difference.

In early philosophical writings, individualism and the interests of the individual were seen as being in opposition to the interests of the community. The anthropological evidence, however, indicates that human beings were always social animals, and the historical evidence suggests that individualism is rooted in family, in community, and in service. In the biographies of many famous individualists, organizations like the Boy Scouts are cited for building a sense of self-worth and a sense of service.

With the migration to the cities, community ties were severed and community involvement and service correspondingly declined. This created the climate in which the perversion of individualism called "me-ism" arose. With a diminished role for young people in helping their families and with fewer opportunities to make a real difference in their communities, self-interest became, for many, the only remaining motivation. Getting more stuff became the proof of self-worth. We lost the concept of the common good. This could prove to be fatal. The kind of individualism that pioneers the human journey is not a phenomenon of increased selfishness; it is, instead, a phenomenon of greater consciousness, stronger convictions, greater courage, and increased contribution.

DETRIMENTAL ORGANIZATIONAL FORCES

For almost two centuries, organizations were toxic environments for individualism. Individualism was only well-suited to craft and agricultural economies. Individualists did things their own way, took the time to do them right, were constantly experimenting with ways to do them better, cared that the fruits of their labor benefited others, and adopted "natural" schedules. Not popular behaviors for bureaucracy, and downright unworkable for mass production. Therefore, individualism was basically stifled.

But for almost 30 years now, there has been a growing movement, although somewhat misguided, to turn this around. The requirements of organizations changed and new behaviors were needed. Voices came from several fields—industrial psychology, adult education, organization development, human resource development, human resources, quality management, and management consulting. Many pioneering organizational leaders led the change effort, particularly in the high-tech and information industries, and in hotels and retail, with their intense interest in customer satisfaction. The main threads have been about involvement, empowerment, and ownership.

Still, the focus has not been on individualism itself, and many organizational improvement efforts, though beneficial in other ways, continue to discourage and suppress individualism. Look again at the behaviors of individualism described above. Add to those the fact that individualism is particularly well-suited to uncertain and changing conditions—individualists do not discourage easily, and they *will* find a way. Most of us would agree that these are desirable and needed behaviors in today's highly competitive, innovation-driven environment. Focusing on the organizational forces detrimental to individualism will help us find ways to hasten its return to serve the pioneering our organizations need.

Management Controlled

Increasingly, managers have been able to manage larger and more complex enterprises, with relatively consistent positive results.

Predictability and control have been hallmarks of this effort. These concepts continue to be important, but without modification, they produce some unintended negative consequences. One of those negative consequences is the discouragement of individualism.

Here are some examples. The standardization of work, while very productive under certain conditions, has been frequently criticized as a factor limiting individual initiative and pride in workmanship. Objectives, while aiding us in managing more complex endeavors, also silenced the campfire stories of individual brave deeds and daring tactics. The objective impersonality of job descriptions and performance appraisal took their toll. And perhaps worst of all is that leadership too often has meant being cognitive enough and cold-hearted enough to "downsize" by the numbers, giving little attention to the individuals who have made a difference in the past and who could do so in the future.

I witnessed a wonderful exception to this trend in the early days of Texas Instruments. A cantankerous but highly gifted machinist who had grown up with the original company, Geophysical Services Inc., would not have fit into the new, standardized mass production environment. But due to his legendary accuracy and the advocacy of a few managers, he was given his own shop in the new Central Research Laboratories. It was a brilliant move. He could make anything, to the tightest tolerances, quickly—a real gift in fabricating custom lab equipment. And his personality equipped him perfectly for dealing with the equally individualistic research scientists. It is likely that some of the pioneering research that emerged from the Central Research Labs would not have been possible without his accuracy, and it is almost certain that it would have taken light years longer.

Teamed Up On

In the last decade, the effort to develop teams—a worthy undertaking—was also accompanied by a tendency to suppress individualism. In attempting to copy the kinds of teamwork found elsewhere, individual self-interests were often regarded as antisocial and individually held opinions that had not been cleansed by consensus were considered antithetical to teamwork. While there may be granules of truth in this, they are not grains. In the West, and particularly in the United States, any attempt to develop teamwork at the cost of individualism will likely produce "go-along" passivity and something short of breakthrough results. We must actually build teamwork firmly on the foundation of individualism.

Unfreedom of Speech

Political correctness and its attendant legal actions have weakened the expression of convictions. Its goal of eliminating bias unfortunately was driven by an equal bias that leveled such a barrage of accusations and sanctions that only the most courageous were not intimidated. Many have come to believe that it is more important, or at least more prudent, to understand the other person's point of view than it is to stand up for their own. The pressure to fit in and to follow fads has been just as devastating. A compulsion for consensus has added to the toll. Organizations need to revive the fine art of debate. These debates may not always be civil. A lack of conflict often means that nobody cares enough to fight for their convictions.

Making Self-interest a Bad Word

One of the ironies of our time has been the efforts of self-interested managers to discredit self-interest. It has become fashionable to act as if self-interest is a form of disloyalty and should not be considered in deciding what to do and how to do it. Of course, this usually refers only to the self-interests of those lower in the chain-of-command. This tendency is particularly notable under the banner of the cost-reductions needed to stay competitive. The most pernicious forms appeal to the employees' fear of losing their jobs and attempt to enlist their genuine desire to make a contribution. These would be legitimate if at the same time the leaders contained their own costs.

While individualism is largely not about self-interest, it nonetheless includes it. Self-interest is at the core of self-reliance and is the antidote to attitudes of entitlement and victimhood.

When cost-reduction and containment efforts are built firmly with individual self-interests in mind, employees often find better, cheaper, faster ways to do things and achieve amazing results because they also believe their interests are being served. The example of Delta employees some years back comes to mind. Not only did they find ways to cut costs and increase sales in order to avoid layoffs and salary reductions, but they chipped in and bought the company an airplane as well.

Perhaps a definition for organizations will help us see the central role of individual self-interest in the performance of organizations. *Organizations are people working together to achieve mutual and reciprocal purposes.* There is not just one purpose, the organization's purpose, but there are also the purposes of the individual men and women who agree to work there. Those purposes are clearly about self-interest. When these interests are ignored, made undiscussable (except in union negotiations), or endangered, clearly a great deal of the energy needed to produce extraordinary results is gone.

Packaged and Shipped

Human resource systems, in an attempt to bring order and fairness to employment, compensation, and promotion, have weakened individual initiative and self-reliance. Far too many organizations continue to be burdened by cumbersome, outdated classification systems and selection processes that consume inordinate amounts of time. The organizational needs of creating new priorities, moving talent to the task, and ganging up on emerging opportunities are tangled in a web of bureaucracy. Employee skills are shrink-wrapped in arcane categories, and employee agility is shackled by a maze of application procedures. We need entrepreneurial e-systems—something like "competency cards" that are coded with skill data, education, and experience. Such systems could enable employees to move quickly to opportunities, make their own cases for what they can contribute, and free up project leaders to pick their own teams. The current systems designed for fairness too frequently take the form of punishing everyone equally.

Leadership Ambivalence

Organizations begin as a pioneering act. Someone or some few decide that a certain purpose or purposes would be better served if people came together in an organized and ongoing way to work toward their achievement. These are the founders of the organization. Usually they are strong individuals and individualists. It could be argued, therefore, that developing, maintaining, or rekindling this pioneer spirit would be a goal. It is also reasonable to expect that the goal could be best served by attracting, developing, and maintaining individualism within the organization, and not just at the top. Seldom is this the case.

Furthermore, most large organizations are characterized by top managers who are individualists. Too often, however, they encourage teamwork only for those below them and discourage individualism. Even the best managers often show a certain ambivalence toward the emerging individualists in their midst. While they may champion and sponsor a few themselves, they frequently question the judgment of those reporting to them when they tolerate the antics of individualists in their units. At a time when more individualists are needed in a great many more positions, this severely restricts the supply chain.

Downsizing, Outsourcing, and the Signing Bonus

These are some of the most frequently used tools in modern management. Each of them has played a vital role in the survival and success of many top companies. Each of them has benefits for most of the organization's stakeholders—customers, shareholders, vendors, managers, the communities in which the companies operate, and even for employees. Downsizing saved many employee jobs. Outsourcing created new jobs in smaller companies. And signing bonuses and stock options have created many employee millionaires. There is reason for concern, however, about their collective impact on individualism.

The first major use of downsizing came in some of the world's most stable and dependable organizations. It was not just the result of market swings. It had long-term implications. It signaled the beginning of a new era in employment practice. No longer could employees expect to work for a single employer throughout their careers. No longer was there a real rationale for employee loyalty. The sense of belonging—one of the five strengths of individualism—that had been provided by these organizations for those who had left their community roots was gone forever. It was gone for those who parted; it was gone for those who stayed.

Outsourcing, of course, picked up much of the slack and created jobs for most of those who had been separated. The growth of opportunity for small spin-off companies has been one of the success stories of our time. It more than corrected for the lack of promotional opportunity that was beginning to plague many larger and older organizations, and it stimulated the entrepreneurial spirit. The number of CEOs multiplied dramatically. The boon to the U.S. economy is obvious. But the sense of belonging did not return. In fact, a certain restlessness seemed to grow in the heart of individualism. It was now possible for individualists to go their own way again, to reclaim some lost seeds of self-reliance. "If it doesn't work out here, then I can simply go on to the next opportunity." Signing bonuses and lucrative stock-options have added to this trend.

So what is the loss? Perhaps there is none. Perhaps it is simply an evolution in the history of individualism—a way to make a contribution and still be one's own boss, much as it was on the frontier or on the farm. Perhaps it is a stimulus to individualism and will be one of the forces that aid in its return. Perhaps it is the beginning of global individualism. But there is reason for concern.

On the front page of the *Austin American-Statesman*, the leading daily in Austin, on Sunday, August 22, 1999, one of two lead stories that day was an article about such opportunistic restlessness. It explained how stock-option signing incentives had become the reason for rapid job-hopping, the means for attempting to strike it rich with a successful IPO—a new form of wild catting. "My golden rule is evaluate every six months, and if you're not going to be associated with success, move on," one start-up VP was quoted as saying.

Have we created a new form of employment and a new form of organization, or have we created the virus that will decimate all organizations? If no one has a sense of belonging, to what will be the contribution? Will the world of work be populated only by free agents, temporaries, mercenaries, and consultants? Will there be enough cohesion and time for any pioneering in the age to come? I believe the solution to these problems can come from a new kind of individualism—interdependent individualism—in the service of convergent organizations.

THE RISE OF INTERDEPENDENT INDIVIDUALISM

Up to now, the picture of individualism I've presented has been of dignified, upstanding, somewhat distant, and independent behavior—a kind of New England stereotype. But individualists are more often helpful, engaged, full of ideas and suggestions, eager to help, not easily offended, and seldom bored. They may be either optimists or pessimists, but once they have voiced their doubts and concerns, if the decision is made to go forward, they will do their best to make it happen. You can count on them. People who know their own minds and are willing to act on their convictions make the strongest, most dependable commitments.

Individualism has always been rooted in community. The conditions of the American frontier spawned an appropriately *independent* form of individualism. But such individualists were quick to help their neighbors. These independent people came together frequently to raise barns and to harvest crops. This quality applies generally. Because of their interest in understanding things for themselves, individualists tend to be unusually aware of the developments, needs, and possibilities of their times. They respond to those needs, serve them, and take advantage of them. It is my conviction that the intense interconnection of the modern world is giving rise to a new *interdependent* form of individualism.

Consider the people in your organization. The "Marlboro Men" are not the individualists of our time. They do not think. They spend a lot of time hanging out with guys who have the same opinions as theirs. They support each other in stereotyping, sarcasm, and in shifting responsibility. Despite its legitimate criticism of such men, sisterhood is frequently guilty of the same sins.

The individualists in your organization are the ones who are leading teams. They are the ones seeking win-win solutions. They are the ones offering support in getting the job done. They are the ones willing to surface differences and disagreements and to stay in the room until they are resolved. In personal life, since they know themselves and are secure in their identities, they are the ones most capable of intimacy.

The word individualism begins with *in*. As in going within, but also as in entering in. As in being involved and committed. As in using your intelligence. It is about looking for your part in the matter, rather than placing all the blame on others. It is about inner awareness, not just statistical information. And finally, it is about intention and integrity.

At Vignette, there is a great deal of attention to the company's declared and printed values about its customers, the kind of business it wants to be, and its expectations of itself as an organization of people. On the list are several "in" words. Integrity appears twice. Others are: "Quality *in* everything we do. Individually behaving like you are in business for yourself. Fostering an innovative environment. And finally, intellectual honesty." This is not unlike the values being advocated by many other organizations today. Conditions call for them. These are not the values of selfishness, stubbornness, and separate agendas. They are the values of interdependent individualism.

THE NEED FOR A NEW KIND OF INDIVIDUALISM AND A LOT OF IT

Today's jobs simply call for a lot more individualism, and yet higher levels of teamwork are also required. The nature of work has changed. A great many more people perform a variety of tasks independently, rather than repeating the same simple task on an assembly line. Yet most of this work is modular and must fit together with the work of others. Many more of the tasks are intellectual, requiring judgment and creativity. More ideas are needed, more intellectual capital. Many more people are in a position to spot opportunities for improvement and to envision new products. The very nature of such work is entrepreneurial. Such jobs cannot be performed by go-along, follow-orders, unthinking employees.

The relationship to customers is also different. Customers' needs are different. No longer is it possible to simply punch out standardized products or to provide one-size-fits-all services. The word *custom* is in the middle of the word *customer*. This calls for a great many real-time, innovative solutions. It also calls for employees who will set aside the accepted way of doing things and even create "new policy" on the fly if it is required to provide what the customer needs. A great many sales are created in the solution, not in the showroom. This requires employees who are not policy-whipped, yes-men and yes-women. It requires people who can think independently and who have the courage to act on their own initiative.

Two other conditions contribute to the need for increased individualism. Individualists are not just better at responding to change: they are change agents. With individualists, we can reduce the budget for change management and increase the budget for change initiatives. Additionally, the kind of teamwork required in today's business environment is not the kind found in team sports, where there is only one ball and only one person at a time can score with the ball. Today's multifaceted marketplace offers opportunities for simultaneous scoring and calls for teamwork that can keep many balls in the air at once. This is interdependent individualism in action. We need a new metaphor.

A CREDO FOR INTERDEPENDENT INDIVIDUALISM
- I need to think things through for myself. There may be a better answer.
- I will have the courage to fight for what I think is right.
- I will do my best to take care of myself and declare my self-interests.

- I realize I am seldom fully independent, so I will strive to avoid arrogance. I realize I am seldom fully dependent, so I will avoid acting like a helpless victim. I understand that most of the time I am interdependent, responsible for myself through cooperation with others.
- I have a can-do attitude. Much of the time, I can do what is needed. When I can't, I will ask for the help I need to get it done.
- I will be accountable. It is up to me. I will avoid hiding behind excuses, a team, a job description, a bureaucracy, or Human Resources.
- I often think I have a better idea, and I will fight for it, but I will also listen to others.
- I will always try to make a difference.

For many of you, this credo should sound familiar. It is descriptive of a great many pioneering individuals of all cultures who have cleared the path for others. The values embodied by such people make it clear that the "get mine me-ism" of the '80s was not individualism, but merely selfishness.

While it may not be developed, the impulse toward interdependent individualism is inherent in all people. It is natural. We are born with it. It starts with the drive in every little kid to see what she can do and to show others he can be counted on. Just after the "I can do *that* myself" of the two-year-old comes "Let me help." From the first, self-interest is tied closely with service. We demonstrate our competence in order to build our feeling of self-worth *and* to build in others a sense of confidence in our worth to them.

If it is not suppressed, this drive produces a person who sees what needs to be done and does it, rather than waiting to be told what to do. In a healthy culture, this even applies to teenagers. In fact, at other times in history, teen years were the age at which such individualism expanded beyond contributions to the family into service for the community.

As individualism matures, both self-interest and service enter into a deeper quest for meaning and purpose. Individuation and shouldering the responsibility to provide for one's own needs are part of the development of healthy individualism. But making a difference and being of value to others is too. It is natural to want to be able to take care of oneself. It is also natural for people to *want* to make a contribution—to make a difference in the lives of those around them. This naturally aligned motivation provides an inherent basis for true teamwork, and tapping it does far more than all the recent fad techniques for teams.

So why has individualism been feared and frequently suppressed? For much of human history, resources were scarce, danger was everywhere, and change was slow. People needed to pull together and work was mostly physical. New ideas were unwelcome. They might put the entire community at risk. Leaders were expected to protect the community and to control deviant behavior. Individualism of any kind was a luxury society did not feel it could afford.

But we are on the threshold of a promising future for the human race. The benefits gained in the march of individualism can be extended to all people everywhere. Global prosperity is possible, and we can heal the damage to our environment as we achieve it. Yes, there is danger, but there is also opportunity. The recent suppression of individualism came not because it presented a danger to the community, but because it presented a threat to the greed of a few. And it was carried out by leaders controlled by those greedy few.[6] Individualism can lead the way to a better future for all, but it must be empowered by a new breed of leaders, leaders who have a pioneering vision and work in behalf of us all. Convergent leadership is required for us to gain the benefits that come from the rise of interdependent individualism.

This leadership will be discussed further in Chapter 6, but for now, here is a short outline of things leaders can do to help create organizational conditions that facilitate and support the development of the five strengths of individualism. Leaders can:

- Establish a new basis for *belonging* by opening real ownership to all and by designing financial strategies that favor long-term employment. At Vignette, where all employees own stock, CEO Greg Peters describes a new program they launched to *retain* their employees in the future. "We are in great shape now," he says, "but four years from now, many of our best and brightest may be tempted to leave us for the entrepreneurial opportunities of start-up ventures. We decided to find a way to give them that opportunity while staying with Vignette. So we created the V.I.P. program." Vignette invested an initial $50 million for the year 2000 in other venture software companies with products or technologies they need to supplement their current offerings. Without any cost to them, Vignette employees will receive 50% of the gains. These gains will be paid quarterly *after 4 years of employment.* "All employees participate," Peters says, "except for the muckety-mucks. They do not even need to sign up."

- Encourage the continuing development of *inquiring, independent thinking* by expanding the practice of inviting the critique and vision of all.

- Support people who show the *courage of their convictions* by surfacing all doubts and concerns and encouraging authentic and complete debate before consensus. Also, lessen some of the dangers by putting the reins on the overuse of political correctness and politeness.

- Bolster *self-reliance* by expanding the freedom of entrepreneurial action and encouraging risks.

- Strengthen *self-esteem*, satisfaction, and meaning by expanding opportunities for customer and community service and by embracing a pioneering vision.

DEVELOPING INTERDEPENDENT INDIVIDUALISM IN HOUSE

An unprecedented need for individualism has emerged in the organizations of the post-industrial world. This has become particularly apparent given the explosive growth in information technology jobs, and it has reached crisis proportions with the warp-speed spread of the Internet. To put it simply, thousands of companies are competing for an incredibly scarce resource.

The problems of today's job market have been understood in terms of a shortage of people with the necessary *technical* qualifications. But the real problem is finding technically qualified people who think independently, have the courage to act on their ideas, and who are self-directed and self-starting. What organizations are seeking are individualists. Furthermore, we need individualists who can work effectively with others, who will make a commitment to our cause, and who will stay with the company long enough to make a valued contribution. We need *interdependent* individualists. And we need them urgently.

It will not be possible to put a Band-Aid over the problem with signing bonuses alone. We must find out how to develop these capacities in the people we already have on board and to develop organizations that support them. This will require real understanding. Superficial, flavor-of-the-month programs will not do it. The capacities of interdependent individualism require high-order skills. Developing them will require high-order leadership.

Individualism is characterized by a lifelong quest for competence and for making a contribution. The human journey toward self-reliant competence is itself a form of pioneering. It requires much the same spirit. Individualists also want to make their lives count for something. They seek better ways of doing things. They tend to become discontent with the status quo. They believe they can make a difference and that their ideas can be a contribution to the benefit of all. They are willing to stand up for their ideas and to risk the consequences of disapproval. All of these are what fuel the pioneering spirit.

Teamwork as Aligned Individualism 5

*T*he critical factor for organizations is teamwork, not teams. Work is organized as systems that cross many teams, not as discreet sets of tasks for work units. Strengthening teams often results in stronger boundaries between units and therefore in tougher turf protection. Strong unit teams may result in production gains within those units, but will frequently produce a net loss across the entire system due to conflicts between the teams. In addition, when the focus is on the output of work unit teams, managers must carry the whole load of bringing these outputs together in a coordinated fashion. There are not enough hours in a day for managers to do that in complex systems. Teamwork throughout systems, in all directions, and planned and executed by everybody is what is needed. This kind of teamwork can be defined as *an attitude of mutual commitment in which everyone takes responsibility for the overall results, not just for their individual contributions or those of their work groups.*

We seek teamwork in order to accomplish things together that we cannot accomplish alone. Again, this is about teamwork, not teams, so we won't talk about bonding, developing more meaningful relationships, fuller humanity, group therapy, individual therapy, or self-discovery. All of those are valuable pursuits, but their contributions are not essential for teamwork in the workplace. Teamwork on the job only requires that we decide what we are going to do together, how we need to help each other in getting it done, commitment to our plan of action, and ways to deal with problems when they arise. Doing those things well, however, also requires certain principles and skills.

For effective teamwork to exist, two beliefs and two commitments are required. Those involved must believe in and be committed to what they are trying to achieve and how they will work together to achieve it—*a purpose commitment*. They must also believe in each other and be committed to cooperating in doing whatever it takes to accomplish their purpose—*a mutual responsibility commitment*. Such commitments are dependent on how leadership and the organization deal with a number of critical issues. Those issues are discussed later in this chapter.

THE BENEFITS OF TEAMWORK

There are many benefits that come from committed teamwork. A partial list follows:

More Muscle

The earliest forms of teamwork made use of the combined muscles of many people to move objects that even Sampson could not move alone. For this to be effective, however, coordination was required. Unfortunately, this was the role that led to a great deal of slavery. The pyramids were built on this kind of teamwork. So were the agriculture and mining industries. Today, in the world of work, machines have replaced much of the need for physical teamwork. Sports and domestic life are its remaining domains.

More Eyes

This form of teamwork involves using more pairs of eyes to observe what is happening, to observe different points of the action simultaneously, and to modify plans accordingly. It was part of the secret of man's success in hunting and gathering. It made it possible to sail large ships and to scout out danger in crossing the prairie. To gain this teamwork benefit, however, people must be able to communicate what they are seeing and listen to each other's reports. Today, visual teamwork, aided by the extension of artificial eyes, is important in managing an assembly line, running a railroad, and pioneering space. Since customer needs exist in many locations and at many levels of today's organizations, more eyes are crucial in finding the business opportunities that exist. For most people, a vision about how something could be better originates in the eyes.

More Perspectives

Teamwork gives us the ability to consider things from many different perspectives. Our chances of understanding the truth of any situation are greatly enhanced by this. For this benefit to occur, people must be willing to hear other people's perspectives and to consider them as potential *aspects* of the truth. It is still crucial, however, for individual human beings to assess situations for themselves and to form their own opinions. Remember, individuals are the locus of organizational commitment.

More Ideas

In deciding how to do things or how to solve a problem, it is useful to have more ideas than one person can have. It is also important to have a range of ideas from which to choose. Again, for this kind of teamwork to pay off, people must be willing to consider each other's ideas.

More Information

This was one of the main reasons for creating think tanks. Many different specialties were included. Today, with the vast quantities of information available on the Internet, the emphasis on this kind of teamwork is diminishing. We may pay a price, since there is a tendency to go with superficial, unverified, sound-bytes of information.

More Time

Through the use of teamwork, it is possible to operate 24 hours a day.

Coordinated, Committed Implementation

This is the most common need for teamwork in organizations today. The lack of it is also the source of most problems.

Sustained Spirit

All of us have our ups and downs. With committed teamwork, someone can always step forward to revive our spirits.

In the end, though, beyond its benefits, teamwork is necessary because it is not just a desirable behavior. It is, in fact, the essence of organization, of people coming together to help each other accomplish a common cause they could not have accomplished alone. So working toward desirable teamwork behaviors is essential.

A CREDO FOR TEAMWORK

- I will seek to develop teamwork in all directions.
- We must first take time to get clear on what we are trying to do, how we will do it, and who will do what. Agreement and commitment are essential.
- I will tell others truthfully what I am willing and able to do. When I cannot do what is needed, I will look for other ways to be helpful.
- I will strive to achieve our mutual purpose. When problems arise, I will be open about my concerns and doubts, take seriously the concerns and doubts of others, and work with them to resolve our differences.
- They can count on me to do what it takes to reach our shared objectives. We are each fully accountable for the final outcome.

In the *Credo for Teamwork* presented above, some of the commitments are natural, but some of them are not. Working together to accomplish a common agenda and taking mutual responsibility for the outcome are both natural human behaviors. Being open about concerns and doubts and being completely truthful about intentions and ability are difficult and consequently *do not usually occur without help and hands-on leadership.*

A few of the natural tendencies associated with teams even get in the way of teamwork. For example, the natural human needs for affiliation and community often degenerate into a desire to fit in and be accepted. These take counterproductive forms, such as people pleasing, going along, and caving in to peer pressure. Lynch mobs, gangs, and complacent conformity are sad testimony to such tendencies.

Even the outlaws of the Old West demonstrated a need to be accepted and recognized—they traveled in gangs, and not just for firepower. Unfortunately, their need for peer approval frequently took the form of showing how mean and vicious they could be. One top management group I worked with devoted a lot of their meeting time to showing each other they were the toughest predators around—lone wolves needing no one, caring for no one. They were all extremely well paid. Still, in private interviews, they were nearly unanimous in indicating that one of the things they wanted most was the recognition and regard of their peers. More bluntly, they wanted to be liked, and their tough predator talk was their way of trying to be accepted by the group.

It takes a great deal of courage or a great deal of trust for people to risk losing the acceptance of their peers. When they voice doubts and concerns, or when they critique the group's work, they risk just such a loss. They also risk it if they speak truthfully about what they can and cannot do. So generally, they are inclined to mumble agreement to the group's plans and to collude in finding excuses and external scapegoats when things don't work out. Strong individualism is the best cure for this malady.

Many of the techniques used in recent team building programs did little to change this natural bonding/bending behavior. Personality and diversity training made it easier to discuss individual differences of opinion and preference, but often made it even

93

more difficult to candidly critique performance and to deal with issues of individual commitment and competence. Some of the meeting and planning techniques advocated particularly by Total Quality Management helped in getting work issues on the table, but tended to ignore or gloss over issues arising from self-interests or from feelings that some were not carrying their share of the load. Furthermore, the statistical techniques might pinpoint a trouble spot in production processes, but did little to move interdependent functions away from blame and toward collaboration. This required more than numbers, it required trust. But most of the techniques aimed squarely on solving trust problems focused on the wrong kind of trust. Trusting someone to catch you on a ropes course is quite different from trusting someone's intentions and competence to do what is needed on the job.

To make matters worse, the focus of the recent fad was on "teams," not on *teamwork*. Teams became almost mystical as, time after time, the stories were told of legendary teams like the Green Bay Packers of the '50s or the WWII Lockheed team that designed a bomber in a weekend. Either in origin, in membership, or in mission, these legendary teams often benefited from factors that did not exist in the typical teams at work. A lot of thought and effort went uselessly into trying to understand how to recreate the special chemistry of such teams, rather than simply identifying the specific acts of teamwork needed to accomplish certain objectives and then gaining agreement to work together in the needed ways.

Developing strong teams had some other unintended negative consequences. On many of these teams, the peer loyalty aspect began to "dumb down" or "norm down" performance expectations. Lazy or less competent team members tended to band together and to have hallway conversations with their more ambitious colleagues (or to covertly report them to HR). Being a good "team player" frequently meant defending the team against outsiders, which were often other teams who had a stake in the outcome and sometimes even customers. A new strain of team "protectionism" emerged that often raised the barriers between teams and across functions rather than lowering them. This despite all the cross-functional talk to the contrary.

Such team cultures also tend to suppress individualism. It becomes a "no-no" to speak up in ways that draw attention to oneself and might make one a candidate for additional recognition or reward. Critiquing the team's performance, particularly in any public forum (one involving anyone other than team members), is clearly a cardinal sin. Interviews indicate a significant backlash building to "teams" due largely to such oppressive tendencies. That is the basis for at least some of the groans heard when people are asked to be on yet another team.

A focus on *teamwork*, on the other hand, does not depend on understanding an esoteric formula and avoids these unintended consequences. Teamwork is a natural human inclination that takes very little to call forth. It is difficult to describe the essence of a team, but it is quite easy to describe the kinds of teamwork that will be needed to achieve a particular goal. It is also easy to describe the principles. The credo above contains most of them. As such, focusing on teamwork, rather than teams, is both more concrete and more actionable.

THE STEPS OF EFFECTIVE TEAMWORK

The simple steps for effective teamwork are as follows:

1. Decide what to do together and how to do it.
2. Clarify how each will help, what each needs from the other.
3. Declare self-interests.
4. Specify the resources needed from others, and request them.
5. Work through trust issues; develop tangible agreements that enhance and maintain trust.
6. Design appropriate processes for every kind of teamwork that will be required.
7. Agree on ways to measure progress and resolve any problems that arise.

Some of the competencies that are needed become apparent just by reviewing the steps. Clearly, good communication skills are required. In post-industrial organizations, understanding systems and the skills for solving problems are essential. An understanding of basic business math is a big plus. It is crucial to be open about any concerns and competing interests that could affect commitment. And for teamwork to achieve optimum levels of effectiveness, everyone involved needs to have the skills for handling disagreement and for asking for what they want.

Not only are these the skills of teamwork, but these are supremely the skills of interdependent individualism as well. Leaders especially need to have these competencies, and they need to create a culture in which these skills are expected and welcome.

MISSTEPS

A Compaq assembly line supervisor told me of some things he learned while working on an assembly line elsewhere. He had a college degree and a great deal of experience at the time, having just retired from the Air Force at a young age. Because of other interests, he had wanted night shift work, and the assembly line job came with the promise of quick promotion. He swallowed a few feelings he had about the work being beneath him and decided to look at it as a learning experience. He was surprised at just how much he learned, and more pointedly, *what* he learned.

He had expected the routine and the monotony. What he had not expected was the way little things co-workers said or did at breaks started to take over his mind when he was back on the line. It didn't matter how he tried to control his mind, or how much he believed it was small stuff, or that such things had never bothered him before. Given the unrelenting monotony of the job, he found himself upset, irritated, and sometimes very angry. When he became a supervisor, this knowledge aided him greatly in dealing with worker concerns that arose in that kind of environment.

Perhaps this story sheds some light on some of the methods many have employed over the last 20 years in attempting to develop teamwork. Those methods may have responded to the routine, bureaucratic, authoritarian nature of the organizations that existed 20 years ago. Usually the issues between people were not about work: those matters were dictated by the machines. They were usually about hurt feelings. Given that, our methods were perhaps understandable, even though many of them were missteps even then.

Given the very different nature of most work today, however, several of those methods are inappropriate, ineffective, misplaced, and even harmful. Some of the methods get sidetracked by making sympathy, nurturing, and comfort their main business, but that's the job of parents, friends, and marriage partners. Seeking that in work relationships is neither good for the team nor for the individual. Other mistaken methods are actually concealed attempts to right social injustices and have very little to do with developing what is needed for effective teamwork. Instead of confronting groups of workers with these larger problems, what is needed is for top management to eliminate social injustice in their organizations and to help the government do so in society as a whole.

When the steps of teamwork described above are followed, most of the problems that such methods were designed to correct simply go away. For example, most people become blind to personality, culture, and gender differences when they have reached an agreement about how they will help each other do what is needed. If we need to pull together to meet a critical deadline, if the fate of the organization depends on it, it is not important to me that you are an ENFP—an Extrovert, Intuitive, Feeling, Perceiving personality type (according to the Myers-Briggs personality types). Just pull hard, please.

TEAMWORK AS ALIGNED INDIVIDUALISM

Given the kinds of teamwork needed by organizations to be successful in the 21st century, aligned individualism, rather than strong teams and team theory, offers a better answer. Such teamwork strengthens our resolve and energizes our efforts. When it is healthy, it supports individuality. Paradoxically, healthy interdependence enhances our independence. Through teamwork, our self-reliance is bolstered. Through service to others, we gain self-esteem. It is important to be counted on by others. These companionship needs are best met by pulling together when the going is hard and by celebrating our victories when we win. Rather than sensitivity sessions, the simple practice of requesting what we want and of appreciating others for what they give makes all of this possible.

At Collective Technologies, aligned individualism, as the basis for teamwork, is the organizing principle of the organization. The consultant system administrators are recruited to work alone, encouraged to act as entrepreneurial individualists out-stationed in their own client companies, but they work together via e-mail and converge on each other's sites when needed. They call this collective intellect.

Ed Taylor, CEO at Collective Technologies, tells this story of the company's California employees. One of the consultants, a systems administrator in an organization on the coast of California, sent out an urgent e-mail one evening around 9 p.m. He described a problem he had run into that he did not know how to fix. He had a response within seconds from a colleague, a consultant on a completely different assignment, about a hundred miles down the coast. They worked together by e-mail (a chat room open to all of the company's consultants nationwide), but did not immediately find a solution. At about 11 p.m., this near-neighbor Collective colleague showed up at the door, pizza in hand. Colleagues stationed in other companies were joining in on the e-mail collaboration by this time.

The two consultants onsite joined in the "discussion" while munching on their pizza, and later whatever vending machine junk they could find. They tried the solutions the group came up with. No one had encountered a problem like this before, so it took awhile. By the early morning hours, six Collective consultants were working fervently to solve this new problem. By 7 a.m., the exhausted "team" of six had the system up and running. Before going home to pass out, the two onsite employees documented their problem and solution in the company's knowledge repository. They are not obligated or paid to do that, but did it anyway for the sake of the collective intellect.

Teamwork of this kind does not have to be "trained." People know how to do it. And in companies like Collective, where job descriptions and compensation practices don't get in the way, employees do it naturally with pleasure and a sense of satisfaction. No bonding is required; they do not even need to know each other well. It simply feels good to be part of a winning team effort.

This kind of teamwork can also emerge when there are significant and potentially divisive issues. A recent example of this occurred at Classic Communications, which was only six months into a merger of two cable companies of approximately equal size. Three levels of the management team, minus the CEO and CFO cofounders, who were tied up on Wall Street in the last stages of a successful IPO, converged on the company's operations center in Tyler, Texas, to hammer out the first annual consolidated budget. Even though the merger had gone harmoniously up to this time, a number of touchy issues had not yet been worked through, and they were all coming forward in this budget process.

Attendance was more or less voluntary, but everyone was there, given the stakes. To make matters worse, the accounting systems had not yet been consolidated and the software was giving everyone fits. Data was entered. The numbers were coming out crazy. And everyone was helping everyone just try to straighten it out. Days and long nights rolled by, the out-of-towners were definitely needing a change of clothes. By the time the "score" was first added, there was still some significant cutting to do and hard decisions to be made, but "teamwork was already well-established," as Ron Martin, the executive vice president for operations, put it. I don't know how it happened, even though I was watching, but somehow, as Martin, and Mark Rowe, the comptroller, put up target numbers, one small adjustment at a time, none of which were debated or directed, the group achieved the revenue and cost targets. The typical battles that plague most acquistions and mergers had simply not materialized. When the group disbanded, it was time to go home for Christmas. Everyone left in a Christmas spirit. A few weeks later, these numbers passed the muster of investors and Wall Street analysts.

There are many examples of the teamwork of interdependent individualists showing up spontaneously in organizations these days. The nature of knowledge work is that most of this teamwork cannot be led or managed in the old traditional ways. That is the way it has always been on frontiers. The people involved in getting work done across a system must simply get together and talk things through. When facilitation or help is needed, it has very little to do with the traditional team-training curriculum. What is most needed are some good, common sense processes that help organize the discussions so employees can successfully work through the real, sticky issues of deciding what is needed and who will do what. The basic steps are described above. Specific processes and procedures are described in Chapters 7 and 8.

Basically, leaders need to treat employees like they are the smart, willing people that they are—people who can work through all the thorny issues, including the strategic issues of the business. When those issues concern the ways and means of achieving a pioneering vision, the passion of the debate may get hot, but the pleasure of the resolution will be all the more satisfying. Teamwork is instinctive for pioneers. With an understanding of teamwork and interdependent individualism, as well as with an understanding of convergent leadership (Chapter 6), much of the power found in pioneering organizations is explained.

Leadership in the Interest of All 6

L eadership has been the subject of thousands of studies and books. Each month, hundreds of workshops offer leadership training. Millions of managers think of themselves as leaders. But the people who serve under them typically refer to them as boss, manager, officer, section head, or CEO. On rare occasions, someone is spoken of as "our leader." Often, the people who say "leader" have no conscious intent of using a special title of honor; it is just the way they feel. A few, however, say it with pride and speak the words as if they were underlining them. In either case, there is a certain amount of reverence in the voices of those who use the phrase.

Amazing things tend to happen in those departments, squads, organizations, or nations where someone is spoken of as "our leader." History tells of many of them. Joan of Arc was called that by the people of France. Lincoln was given that honor by the citizens of the embattled Union. The men who charged up San Juan Hill said that of Teddy Roosevelt. Winston Churchill was affectionately called "our leader" by his people during the bombing of Britain. And Mother Theresa was referred to as "our mother," but it meant the same thing.

In business, that phrase was used to describe Eric Johnson in the early years at Texas Instruments. It is how Mary Kay is viewed by the thousands of women, and now men, who found new self-respect and undreamed-of prosperity in her organization. In the early days at Apple, a great many bright, young people were drawn to the differing leadership qualities of Wozniak and Jobs. And Hewlett and Packard also received such admiration from the people of their organization. In a different kind of role, Bob Bashor sometimes gets that title from the OD groups he leads at Boeing. From these examples, it would appear that leadership, like beauty, is in the eyes of the beholder.

What did these people have in common? Many of them had a passionate vision. All of them had a compelling sense of mission. And all of them had a *total sense of responsibility for their organizations and the people who served in them.* Convergent leadership is not a new thing, and it is certainly not the fashion. If we are to realize the golden potential of this new millennium, our organizations need to be populated with such leaders.

A CREDO FOR CONVERGENT LEADERSHIP

- I will create an organization that people see as a good place to work. I will dedicate myself to achieving commitment to our vision and earning the trust of our employees.
- I will ensure that throughout the organization there is agreement about what we are doing, how we are doing it, and commitment to our plans.
- I will assure that the organization supports individualism and honors the interests and purposes of every employee.
- I will help develop teamwork in all directions within the organization, with our customers, our vendors, our communities, and our environment.
- I will build a culture of communication and trust. Let it begin with me.
- I will ensure that every process within the organization supports convergence, individual expression, and teamwork in all of our meetings and interactions.

It is sometimes said that the job of top management, particularly that of the CEO, is to create an organization in which people can work together effectively to achieve the organization's goals. This means that organization development, not decision making is the primary task of these leaders. They design and develop organizations in which the people doing the work make the decisions, make good ones, and then do a good job in implementing them. This is a long way from the authoritarian leadership style of making decisions, giving instructions, and watching to make certain employees carry them out.

Bob Young, when he was CEO of Lockheed Engineering & Management Services Company, once emphasized his belief that the organization's culture was his primary responsibility by telling me how he evaluated his own performance. "I will consider myself a success as a CEO the year I make absolutely *no decisions* and the company still does well. Last year I made two." Bob spent most of his time designing the organization and then teaching everyone at all levels how to build it. He would much rather have been giving a workshop for employees and managers than giving orders. The organization did very well.

The six pledges in the credo above are the specifications for organizational development. Taken together, they create a convergence of commitment that powers the organization toward extraordinary performance. The sequence mirrors the process of assessment going on in employee minds that determines the degree of commitment and contribution each will make.

FIRST COMMITMENT: I will create an organization that people see as a good place to work. I will dedicate myself to achieving commitment to our vision and earning the trust of our employees.

The first order of business is to create the kind of organization that inspires extraordinary performance. Creating an organization is about envisioning, designing, forming, informing, focusing, catalyzing, equipping, freeing, facilitating, recognizing, celebrating, and encouraging others by personally doing what they are asked to do. That's what it takes to create an organization that others are drawn to. Picture the men and women who led pioneering expeditions that stirred the imagination of the world. Those are the things they did.

But what exactly is required for people to see an organization as a good place to work? More than a thousand interviews I've conducted as a consultant with people at all levels of organizations would seem to indicate that there are two primary factors. First, they must feel proud to be working there. Their pride comes from believing the organization is doing something worthwhile and they can make a contribution. Second, they must trust the organization's leadership. That trust comes primarily from believing that the leaders are acting in the interests of all.

Feelings of pride and self-esteem come from service, not from self-talk. Employees feel good about the places they work when they believe the organization is doing something that serves people's needs. Employees have a natural motivation toward customer service. When it is missing, most of the time it is because the organization has made customer service difficult or punishing. Such organizations typically are serving the needs of the owners and managers only, and they are attempting to use customers to do so. People do not feel proud to be working in such places no matter how much Wall Street may love them.

Chip Bell tells how at Ritz-Carlton promising new recruits are invited to come visit one of the hotels. Rather than beginning with the traditional interview and tour of the facility, the interviewers simply ask the candidate to spend a day walking around, looking, watching what is going on, and then *looking into their hearts* to see if that is what they want to be part of. The recruits are told before they go on the walk that if they do not feel deeply moved to be part of the Ritz culture and have a sense of joy at the possibility of giving that kind of service, then the Ritz-Carlton is not where they belong. They are assured that Ritz-Carlton will find them a suitable position elsewhere if they do not feel called to be there.

Many people must also believe their organizations are doing no harm. If they believe their places of work are doing harm to the environment or to human health, they may continue to work there and they may even vehemently deny it, but they will not work with commitment. Low performance is the fate of such organizations in today's world. Furthermore, the perception of destructive corporate deeds erodes employee trust, even when they are paid well to participate, by raising the secret fear that those destructive deeds will someday be aimed at them. Usually they are right.

Convergent leaders must work continuously to focus attention on the organization's vision, core values, and challenges. Additionally, they need to call forth the highest vision, best performance, and fullest commitment of every person and team in the organization. At Starbucks, not only do they have large open meetings each quarter for all employees and management in a city, but they also undertake projects in the cities where they operate and in the countries where the coffee is grown that help the people there. Many organizations today involve employees in activities concerning the company's vision. This has been helpful, but it has perhaps become too routine. Signs on the wall lose their meaning. What is needed is for that vision to come alive, to inspire employees to high levels of performance, and to create a culture in which everyone's natural capacity for vision is called forth. Convergent organizations are ones in which all employees are looking for better ways to do things. The company's vision is the foundation for employee pride.

At the Post Ranch Inn, employees have a unique and very tangible way of doing this. Management invites all staff and their significant others to be guests at the Inn once a year. As guests, the employees are received and driven to their luxury cottages ($455 to $755 a night) just as other guests would be. Their cottage is ready with the usual complimentary wine, specialty foods, gourmet coffee and teas, and a refrigerator stocked with all sorts of interesting beverages. Like other guests, they can lounge on private balconies in fluffy, extra-large bathrobes, gazing at the shifting motion of the Pacific a thousand feet below—and gaze through the binoculars at passing sailboats, sea otters, or whales. They can stroll down the path to the spectacular five-star restaurant for sunset and an extraordinary meal. They can relax after dinner in the pool-size spa overlooking the ocean or wait until after the healthy breakfast buffet the next morning. Back in their rooms, they can enjoy a cozy fire and listen to soft music, or they can simply read until they fall asleep in the luxurious covers. All of this so they can find ways to improve the Inn and its service!

New ways of gaining commitment for the company's vision need to be tried. Additional methods are described throughout Part II, or simply create your own out of the special services of your organization.

Let's turn our attention now to what is required for employees to trust the organization's leadership. Leaders have always known that trust in their leadership was the most important factor in people's willingness to follow, but they have not always known what fosters that trust. In the management development program *Straight Talk*[7], Diane Davis and I identified the two factors that most determine trust. The degree of trust we place in someone, it says there, is determined by our perceptions of that person's *intentions* and *competence*. The old folk phrase "willing and able" captures these two factors perfectly.

Many leaders have known intuitively that these were the factors at play and have in various ways attempted to provide reasons why their intentions and competence should be trusted. In their efforts to gain our trust and therefore our votes, political candidates continuously tell us what they *stand for* (their intentions) and point to their records of *accomplishment* (competence). Managers need to find some appropriate ways to do this as well, but far too many think their authority is enough or their competence and intentions are made self-apparent by their position. Certain recent management practices have created a great deal of *mistrust* in the intentions of many CEOs and other top managers. Downsizing to please the stock market and the use of "permanent temporaries" to avoid paying benefits are but two examples.

Since trust is determined by *perceptions*, what can leaders appropriately do that will best demonstrate the trustworthiness of their intentions and competence? The simplest thing is what great leaders have always done intuitively. They do things that simply enable us

106

to see, feel, and sense that they think, act, and speak in terms of the whole and the best interests of all.

Leaders might want to add another commitment to those in the Credo. *I will continuously strive to hold the whole with which I am entrusted in my mind, in my heart, and in my hands. I understand that the trust of those involved is directly proportional to the degree they can feel me holding our individual and collective interests together in this mutual enterprise.* (There was something very trustworthy about that children's song in which the "whole world" was held in capable and committed hands, gender aside.)

"We the people," the Declaration of Independence puts it, " . . . in order to form a more perfect union . . . " " . . . Whether that nation, or any nation so constituted, can long endure . . . ," Lincoln said. He also spoke of " . . . government of the people, by the people, and for the people." The Ritz-Carlton, the Vignette Corporation, Starbucks, and the Post Ranch Inn are all outstanding examples of the spirit of taking responsibility for the whole. At the Post Ranch Inn, general manager Larry Callahan visits everyday with every group of employees to see what they need to get the job done. If employees are experiencing personal problems, he also sees to it that they get the help they need. At Starbucks, Howard Shultz recently told *Executive Excellence Magazine* (November 1999), "I spend a significant portion of my time in trying to touch as many people as I possibly can during the work week. That means visiting lots of stores, walking the halls of our company, communicating via e-mail, communicating in every way possible. I want our people to know how much they are appreciated and to know why the contribution they make each day is so valuable. There is no replacement for being in front of people face-to-face, eyeball-to-eyeball, and communicating the values of our company. ...If our people are not excited, enthused, and passionate about what we're doing, we've got a real problem."

For modern-day corporations, this leadership of the whole must at a minimum include the individuals and teams who do the organization's work, the customers who buy its products and services, the managers who shape its strategies, and the investors holding its stock. It may also be seen to include its vendors, the community in which it exists and does business, and the environment on which it depends. Many recent practices that seem to mostly consider the stockholders, the managers themselves, and sometimes the customers—at the expense of everyone else—are so damaging trust that they may prove fatal to many organizations over time. The appeal to band together against an external enemy (global competition) and the threat of replacing workers with cheaper labor elsewhere will most probably work for only a limited time. There are signs of discontent in many organizations today that indicate time is short. The strikes of 1998 may be an early warning.

"But the cuts were necessary to save the organization and to preserve as many jobs as possible," it is often argued. "Given global competition and cheap labor elsewhere, we have to do everything we can to cut costs." Both of these are valid justifications of some of the management actions alluded to above. Sometimes it is necessary to amputate a leg to save a person's life. But the credibility of these arguments is undercut when downsizing and the structural elimination of jobs become routine management tools, particularly when they are used as a means to manipulate stock prices or when management simultaneously rewards itself with additional bonuses and perks.[8]

Trust and self-sacrifice are forthcoming when leaders are perceived to value the whole in each of its parts, to serve the interests of all involved to the best of their ability, and to share the risks by personally sharing in the consequences—the negative ones as well. If sacrifices have to be made, leaders must also take their places in the line—all of them. Only when top managers also take the hits, not just a few middle managers offered up as symbolic sacrifices, will it be possible to achieve this kind of employee trust.

The recent actions of Norbert Reinhart, owner and CEO of a Canadian mining company, are extraordinary examples. Reinhart, a family man, let himself be taken hostage by Colombian rebels as a replacement for one of his employees, who had been kidnapped by the rebels and was being held as a bargaining piece in getting their demands met by the Colombian government. The employee was free to return to his family and his company job. Reinhart just said he thought it was the right thing to do in his role as CEO of the company.

Thankfully, there are still a few leaders who embody such virtues. Leaders who can hold us all together will be increasingly needed in the 21st century. They'll be chieftains, not warriors. We need to put the "C" back in CEO.

SECOND COMMITMENT: I will ensure that throughout the organization there is agreement about what we are doing, how we are doing it, and commitment to our plans.

Assuring that all are in agreement with plans is leadership in action. This is accomplished increasingly through employee involvement practices. It is time-consuming to do this, but it pays off big. People do not give their best unless they have confidence in what is being done and how it is being done. Most of the time in most organizations, people are holding back. It may be a little or it may be a lot. But even a little holding back can add up to big losses when a lot of people are doing it.

This tendency to hold back does not mean that people are lazy or contrary. Most of them are not. They would like nothing better than the pure joy and satisfaction of giving their all to something they believe in. They hold back, however, because they have unvoiced or unresolved doubts and concerns. Those doubts and concerns focus on what is being done or how it is being done. They lack confidence that the right things are being done in the right ways, or they are concerned that what is being done will not be in their best interests or those of their peers.

Managers tend to suppress such doubts and concerns. They frown on "nay-sayers" and malcontents. One of the most important roles of effective leadership, however, is to continuously surface and resolve such concerns. That is the necessary requirement for achieving high levels of commitment. That is the path to extraordinary performance. To surface and resolve concerns, leaders must treat individual interests and peer group interests as legitimate and honorable. They must also keep employees informed.

Keeping employees informed is widely advocated, but insufficiently practiced. Why? One common and understandable reason is a concern about upsetting the workforce. The unspoken theory is that what they don't know won't hurt the organization. If they knew the facts, it might hurt morale and cause a drop in performance. The truth, however, is that rumors thrive on too little information and are the most frequent cause for employee alarm and lowered performance.

Another reason for keeping information close is a concern for not giving competitors the advantage of knowing your plans. In today's business climate, this is a legitimate concern. Still, if the cost is unaligned performance and low commitment within the organization, this safeguard can be life-threatening. A few years back, Bob Young, a Lockheed CEO, established a company policy of full disclosure, with the only exception being very brief delays—a few days usually—in releasing information at critical junctures of contract procurement. Winning the consolidated contract for space shuttle operations at the Cape was one result of employees having complete information and commitment.

Neil Webber described a similar policy at Vignette. Until recently, all employees were invited to attend executive management meetings on a one-at-a-time, sign-up basis. Practically everyone signed up. Nothing was censored when employees were in the meetings. When it was necessary to guard information for a short time, the employees were asked to keep the information confidential just as the executive managers would do. No one broke this trust. Now that Vignette is a public corporation, it is required to keep financial results confidential until they are publicly reported in the quarterly reports. This and the company's increased size—more than 1,100 employees—is making the practice of one-at-a-time attendance unfeasible. Vignette executives are working to invent a new way to accomplish the high level of disclosure that executive council meeting attendance made possible.

This raises the question of just how wide the scope of employee involvement should be. Managers continue to assume that employee involvement can be limited to specific operational issues or to compartmentalized parts of the business. Beyond that, they assume the employment contract means employees will simply accept management's wisdom about what should be done and do it. It is doubtful that this was ever entirely true, but to the degree that it was, the information age may have changed all that. What is the impact of e-mail, the Internet, and continuous cable news? Have they increased the scope and depth to which leaders need to involve employees in business deliberations?

In most large organizations today, due to the increased availability of information, employees *involve themselves* daily in monitoring and debating the strategic issues facing their companies. They have opinions about these issues. They assess risks and opportunities. They decide just how much commitment they will give to the current plan, just as Wall Street investors decide how much to invest. In other words, they are involving themselves in corporate strategic planning whether the leaders like it or not. In fact, the planning that has the greatest impact may be happening at the water fountains.

Given this state of affairs, it could be argued that leaders need to *involve themselves* in this self-organized employee strategic planning. They might be able to take advantage of these "uninformed" assessments. Instead, I recommend that leaders everywhere begin to find workable ways to involve employees in the strategic issues facing their organizations. Given the power of employee choice to make or break the organization's results, it would seem that leaders would make such involvement a high priority. What's on the table here is performance that is at least 30 percent higher. Those are the results that consistently flow from employee involvement. Job descriptions and performance appraisal can at best result in 70 percent of potential performance. Employees often *choose* to give at least 30 percent more when they feel it is in their best interests or when they believe in the cause.

Beyond discussion, disclosure, and the involvement of employees, effective leaders must exhibit a strong faith in the organization—its mission and its people. This faith does a great deal to allay the doubts and fears of others. Countless stories tell of the power of a leader's faith and confidence. What the stories do not always record is that for the best leaders, confidence is based considerably on facing and resolving as many concerns as possible.

THIRD COMMITMENT: I will assure that the organization supports individualism and honors the interests and purposes of every employee.

This commitment is about seeing each and every individual as the organization's best opportunity to achieve its purpose at that point in the organization. Such ideas became almost extinct with the spread of scientific management theory and practice. Managing by the numbers became a way of life. One result was that there is far too little awareness today that those numbers are produced by individual employees and teams. Sitting at their computers, too many managers get the impression that they themselves are producing the numbers as they push the buttons on their keyboards. It has become the newest video game.

Leaders who have the ability to catalyze extraordinary performance know who is making those numbers happen. They know that the people who are actually doing the "work" are the ones performing odds-defying feats. This knowledge is obvious at Vignette, where they give the software developers and integrators the outside offices with greenbelt and skyline views. The founders and top officers, "the muckety-mucks" as Greg Peters, Vignette's CEO humorously calls the top management group, are in modest windowless offices in the middle. But they don't mind; they're busting with pride. They know that it is individual men and women who make magic happen, and they know many of them, if not all, by name. Convergent leaders are also the ones who value individualists and who find ways to attract and retain a lot of them. They are not threatened by them; they delight in them. These leaders go to great lengths to see to it that their organizations support them. They rally individualism.

Convergent leaders are also personally aware of the needs, interests, and purposes of their employees. They go out and talk with them. At Southwest Airlines, *all* the managers, including all of the top managers, go out and work alongside their employees several times a year. They may not know what each person wants for their lives, but they know the kinds of things each one wants, and they know it because they have taken an interest in employees. It is the manager's responsibility, and they know it.

Perhaps the single most common characteristic of managers who are admired as leaders is the direction of their attention. Far too many managers can be observed referring repeatedly to what is wanted from above and giving most of their attention to meeting those expectations. They are constantly looking up. Some say they are "kissing up." The attention of true leaders (the ones people respond to naturally) is largely on the employees and the customers of their products and services. They are looking out for employee and customer needs. Of course, they still pay attention to aligning the work both laterally and vertically and to achieving exceptional results, but they do so without losing sight of those doing the work and serving their customers. Conversely, managers who spend most of their time attending to expectations from above, even when those expectations are for good customer service, often see numbers rather than customers.

Two more points in this commitment are critical. Too many managers lose sight of two of the deepest human characteristics— human beings are self-serving and meaning-seeking. They have their own purposes aside from what the organization expects, and many of them think there is also a spiritual purpose for their lives. When they join organizations, their purposes come with them. Consequently, people are continuously choosing the endeavors to which they will give their best ideas and fullest commitment. Managers often take this choice for granted. They assume people *should* do what the company needs and what is expected of them from above (management, not God). The result is frequently half-hearted performance and, when possible, job hopping.

Convergent leaders are deeply aware that people have a choice. In recognizing this, however, they are neither passive nor indulgent. They do not stop by finding out what people want; they challenge them to want things that are of great service to themselves and to others. Giving people a choice, or more accurately, recognizing that they are already making choices, is not paternalistic, it is developmental. It develops committed, capable people and tightly linked teamwork. And it develops the highest levels of organizational performance.

FOURTH COMMITMENT: I will help develop teamwork in all directions within the organization, with our customers, our vendors, our communities, and our environment.

Work systems stretch across teams, across organizations, across communities, and across the globe. What is needed in our interconnected world is that those involved take responsibility for what is happening across entire systems, and up and down in the chain of command. It is important that people work together to develop solutions that make the total system work, rather than focusing only on what is good for their team.

Having said all this, however, there is a place for camaraderie, fellowship, and mutual appreciation. Human beings are social animals, and we need this kind of connection with others. It strengthens our resolve and energizes our efforts. When it is healthy, it supports our individuality. Teamwork in all directions is the right expression for this social need. When people all across systems take responsibility for the overall results, everyone benefits and organizations reap the payoffs. At Collective Technologies, the entire organization was designed to support exactly this kind of teamwork. They have produced some miracles in customer service with it (as described in a previous chapter).

Leaders who are working to create the power of convergence in their organizations need to make it clear that they expect this kind of teamwork. They can also facilitate it by making sure all planning includes horizontal, vertical, and diagonal representation. Traditional organizational structure is not a useful forum for planning. Also, this kind of cross-functional planning requires a new kind of leadership skill, one not based on authority or position. This is one of the main uses of OD facilitation in organizations, but more line managers are needed who have the skills. Usually, only a few such managers exist in even large organizations, and they get stretched too thin in today's global economy. The solution is, of course, to provide special training in facilitation skills for line managers.

One thing that works against such teamwork in most organizations is that it does not exist at the top. This is frequently mentioned in the confidential interviews I conduct when I am working to build teamwork in client organizations. When employees perceive that their leaders are playing self-serving, protective games with each other, empire building, or ego competing, they come to believe that this is the way to "play the company game." These perceptions greatly influence what really happens in far too many organizations, in spite of all the appeals for "bringing down the silos" and "lowering the walls." In most companies, protective hedging still far outweighs trusting teamwork. This is certainly a case in which it is crucial for top managers to learn to walk the talk.

FIFTH COMMITMENT: I will build a culture of communication and trust. Let it begin with me.

Trust is the prerequisite for agreement to plans, for teamwork, and for commitment. Communication and a convergence of interests are the sources of trust, not, as is so often asserted, experience. Experience is in fact the cause of much mistrust. And much of that could be avoided or corrected by better communication. Communication is the means we use to seek cooperation in meeting needs—personal needs and the needs of work situations. Making our needs known and being clear about what we are willing and not willing to do, or what we have the ability to do and what we do not—these are the sources of trust. This is the communication needed for tangible trust-building in our organizations. It indicates what is required to find a convergence of interests (see Chapter 9 for more complete information).

SIXTH COMMITMENT: I will ensure that every process within the organization supports convergence, individual expression, and teamwork in all of our meetings and interactions.

Convergent leadership is not about decision making; it is about developing organizations that are good places to work and about ensuring processes that make them that way. Others can invent the products. That's why leaders hire the best specialists they can find. Also, leaders know that everyone needs to help create the strategy and the plan. The unique role for leaders is the organization itself and seeing to it that the organization works effectively in achieving its purpose. That is their business. That is their product. Commitments One and Six are the places they must shine, the places where they not only have final, but also seminal, responsibility.

For pioneering organizations, all processes must work to create convergence. The processes need to enable effective strategy discussions, planning, and execution. Individuals must be able to get their ideas heard and their needs met. For teamwork, processes must make working together pleasant, not punishing. Trust needs to be enhanced, not destroyed by inaccurate information or too little time. Meetings need to be exciting and productive, not dull and draining. Within organizations, things do not happen by chance. They happen as a result of the organization's systems and processes, good or bad. The organizations that succeed in our new century will be the ones that have processes supportive of convergence for all who work in them, all who invest in them, all who use their products and services, and all who are affected by their actions. This is the special calling of convergent leaders.

In conclusion, the first order of business for convergent leadership is the organization itself. Not its products, not the value of its stock, not its marketplace, nor its competitors, its strategy, or its tactics. It is about bringing people together to achieve the organization's purposes and it does so by being aware of *their* purposes and by helping them achieve those purposes. It is about finding a convergence of interests. Organizations are people working together to achieve reciprocal and mutual purposes. Serving the interests of some at the expense of others will no longer do the job.

CREATING PIONEERING ORGANIZATIONS FOR THE 21ST CENTURY

P art 2 goes beyond the characteristics of pioneering organizations, their requirements, and their advantages. It is about creating them. It is about building organizations that will thrive on the challenges of our time—the organizations that will be needed if we are to gain the goal of a golden age for our people and for our planet. It is a program for action that builds progressively toward the extraordinary commitment, excitement, and energy found in pioneering organizations.

The pioneering visions described in the first part began the journey. In today's pressured global economy however, organizations that do not achieve a convergence of interests are not likely to go very far. Part 2 presents a checklist and detailed instructions for working through the six key issues involved in achieving convergence. It describes how to build the exceptional levels of comunication and trust that make convergence possible and how to unleash the energy of commitment required to achieve pioneering breakthroughs. It challenges leaders to examine and change a number of old beliefs that frequently get in the way. And finally, it outlines a rigorous action plan that leaders can use to move their organizations from "business as usual" to peak performance and beyond that to the world-changing power of pioneering.

A Checklist
for Convergence

Work in pioneering organizations often looks like a well-choreographed dance, one with lots of flowing movement, but also throbbing with an energetic beat. Theresa Garza, a corporate VP at Dell Computers, refers to this as "hum." She told *Business Week* in October 1999 that you can feel it as soon as you enter a building. "You can also tell when a company feels dead just by walking through its halls," she said. "We try to create hum. It's people who have momentum, who are working hard, and who are excited to be here."[9]

In pioneering organizations like Dell and Vignette, you can see and feel this energetic dance as people go about their business. A pioneering vision and the commitment that comes from a convergence of the interests of the company with those of the employees is the music that moves this dance. Walking down the halls of far too many other organizations is like watching a funeral march.

There are many competing theories about the critical factors in organizational success. Structure, capital, competitiveness, market fit, resource availability, management skill, adaptability, and creativity, are just a few that are frequently mentioned. None of these is wrong. But the argument of this book is that they are secondary. *Choice is the primary factor.* People *choose* to form or join organizations, and they

121

constantly assess the leadership, direction, and operation of those organizations in *choosing* whether to give or withhold their best ideas and efforts. That is the principle at the core of organizations—the heart of why things happen or do not happen. This chapter provides a checklist of the concerns and issues that are behind that choice. It is a checklist leaders can use to create the convergence and commitment that powers pioneering organizations.

The very definition of organizations makes choice the decisive factor in performance and success. So let's consider the definition of an organization in detail.

Organizations are people working together to achieve mutual and reciprocal purposes.

Organizations are people . . .

The consultants and systems administrators of Collective Technologies who converged in the dead of night to fix a customer problem in California; the master machinist at Texas Instruments; the councilors at the Texas Rehabilitation Commission; the engineers and mechanics at Abbott Labs—these are the people that make up organizations. They are individuals related by purpose— not buildings, machines, products, capitalization, markets, computer networks, or webs. Organizations are not bricks and mortar, nor are they virtual information exchanges. They are the powerful, soft stuff of individual integrity and mutual commitment, supported by intangible things like perception and communication, consciousness and choice, fear and determination.

. . . working together . . .

Working together means feeling arms, legs, hearts, and heads moving as one, doing more, better, faster—counting on each other and being counted on by each other. This phrase underscores the cooperative nature of organizations. Teamwork is the essence of organizations, not something optional.

There are three ways people end up working together: by coercion, by contract, or by choice. Coercion has limited viability today, though unfortunately it is still employed on too many of the world's powerless, tired, and poor. In industrial and post-industrial organizations, the employment contract is assumed to be the primary basis for people working together. I do not dispute that, but I suggest that it accounts for, at best, 70 percent of what happens. Choice is the other 30 percent.

Furthermore, choice initiates and terminates the employment contract. In between, employees constantly assess the organization and its leaders. When employees begin to distrust the organization's direction or its leaders, commitment drops and the choice to do less rises. This choice to hold back frequently impairs 50 percent of an employee's potential to contribute. When employees feel instead that they belong, that they are valued, and that they can create breakthroughs for the human race and for themselves, the pioneering difference emerges.

. . . to achieve mutual and reciprocal purposes . . .

To raise barns and space stations. To make personal dreams come true. To give one's best and to receive it. There is not just one purpose—the organization's purpose. Each person signing on has a purpose, and everyone joining an organization does so with the expectation of helping the organization achieve its purposes while receiving help in achieving their own.

Here are the basic facts about organizations:

- Organizations are formed when various purposes are perceived to be reciprocal and complimentary.

- Organizations perform well when most of those purposes converge and are being achieved.

- Organizations lose performance when people perceive that some purposes are being achieved at the expense of others.

• Organizations disappear when too many people perceive that their purposes are not being achieved.

Pioneering organizations are created when people feel like they are all in it together. Being a "hired hand" does not foster that feeling. Limited involvement and partial participation in decision making may produce higher levels of performance, but not pioneering. Pioneering occurs when people believe they are fully involved in an organization that is creating better possibilities for human life and for their own lives as well.

PERFORMANCE IMPROVEMENT

There are many methodologies for improving employee performance. Compensation, despite the rumors circulated in certain management theories, is still one of the most effective ones. But there are other methods that help. Organizations and employee performance must be understood in terms of the purposes people come there to achieve. The big improvements come when people are given the opportunity to discuss ways in which they can work together more effectively to achieve those mutual and individual purposes.

Specifically, people form or join organizations to increase their personal earnings or earning potential *and* to achieve the organization's financial and service goals. Most people have definite views about ways to achieve both goals. When plans or operations do not correspond with their views, they do not give their best efforts. When, however, they are given the opportunity to express their views, talk through differences, and reach agreement on plans and methods, they commit to *doing* what it takes to achieve them.

Employee involvement and the processes we are about to explore directly address the actions needed for improvement. These processes provide people with an opportunity to consider various alternatives and then choose the ones that best serve all purposes. The agreements that come from this create a situation in which people choose to do their very best. It becomes apparent as you walk through pioneering organizations like Dell that performance "hums." If you listen closely, you will hear that everyone is talking about how to best get things done—they are expressing their ideas and their concerns. The organizations in which people are silently following orders—keeping quiet about their doubts—are the ones that feel like a funeral march.

EMPLOYEE INVOLVEMENT

In the last half century, employee involvement in the management of organizations has increased dramatically. Perhaps the beginning goes back to suggestion boxes. From there, it spread to group involvement in deciding how to do specific jobs, rose to include most aspects of operational planning, and finally ended with participation on "blue-ribbon teams" tackling difficult cross-functional and cross-divisional redesign projects. Some of those involved fundamental business policy issues. By logical extension, it could be argued that employee involvement and choice should now rise to include the discussion and resolution of key strategic business issues.

Any level of inclusion and choice can be very productive, even if the organization is still fundamentally "hired hand." Gains of 50 to 80 percent are not uncommon when techniques such as lean manufacturing, reengineering, team building, kaizen, and other varieties of organizational development are employed. Typically, the technique gets the credit. Leaders all over the planet rush to copy these "world-class" practices. Unfortunately, the magic does not always work in the new setting. The reason is that the results come from employees choosing to contribute better ideas or to work together in more effective ways, not from the technique. The technique merely provides them with a way to make that choice.

For involvement to pay off, it must be in service of a genuine desire to solve problems or produce better results in that organization, not because managers are trying out the latest fad—that only produces cynicism. Leaders who are sponsoring employee involvement projects must have a real intention to work with their employees to find ways to better achieve their shared purposes. Without that, copycat techniques are often as flat as stale beer.

A technique helps, of course. It provides a means for focused discussion, planning, and mutual commitments. The Organization Convergence & Commitment Checklist presented in this chapter, and the action plans found in Chapter 12, include such techniques. But the real magic is not in the technique; it is in people choosing to step forth and give more to the effort. The technique merely provides a structured way for employees to express ideas and concerns and to reach agreements. When commitment increases, it is because employees have found greater alignment between their interests and those of the organization, or they have found credible reasons to do more in the service of purposes in which they believe. Leaders (including those who facilitate such processes) have a large role in establishing conditions that enable this perception of alignment or high purpose to emerge. This is about real things. Charisma, sizzle, and authority alone do not call forth this extra committed effort.

Participation and involvement do not always produce good results. Many mistakes are made, not the least of which is a lack of clarity about the purpose of the involvement. There are two reasons to involve people. One is *competence*, and the other is *commitment*. Letting people make decisions about matters in which they have the most relevant competence seems an obvious thing to do these days, and the results from doing so are consistently high. Attempts to build commitment, however, have less consistent results. That is due partially to activities that are unclear in purpose, but a more common cause for failure is manipulative intentions and techniques. The misuse of a word like *ownership* is an example. When that word is used to describe duty and responsibility without equity and rights, something not too trustworthy is afoot.

Another cause for problems occurs when sincere efforts in parts of an organization are overridden by unilateral management actions further up—often these actions demonstrate the truth about whose interests are being served. Compartmentalized involvement is a variation on this theme. The mandate of too many employee involvement programs is "You can have some say about matters over which you have control—things in your shop—but leave bigger issues to management." There is something circular or redundant about that logic. Giving employees some control over matters in which management says they are accountable might be less twisted logic. But having some say in how the organization serves its customers and having some say in their future prospects with the organization might be a more enlightened policy.

In addition to management-directed involvement initiatives, employees continuously involve themselves. They make judgments about operations based on unvoiced questions, like the following ones found in the Checklist: Are we being asked to do the right things in the right ways? Do I believe the plans will work? Will we get the resources we need to do the job? If we do what they expect, will we benefit—now or in the future? Will my unit support this? Can I trust others to do their part? Will working on this be a rewarding experience, or will it end up being punishing?

Based on assessments like these, made both consciously and subconsciously, employees decide to give their best or to hold back. *That is the most decisive factor in organizational effectiveness today.* Even the most rigorous performance appraisal systems add only incrementally to the results achieved. Employees *decide* whether the results will be "business as usual," less, or more, based on their answers to questions like those above.

In Chapter 6, I argued that employee involvement should include all of the organization's strategies and plans, because employees were making assessments of all of them in determining their commitment and the degree of effort they would give. The Convergence & Commitment Checklist covers all of those assessments and can be used for total employee involvement.

The point is, involvement works, and an increasing number of companies are finding that out. For instance, Saturn bet its success on the idea of involving employees in nearly everything. Employees there design and redesign cars based on their personal experiences in driving them. At Vignette, employees are informed of the financial challenges of the company and given a role in figuring out what to do about them. Some years back, the Texas Rehabilitation Commission (under the guidance of Jimmy Jackson, the COO, and Russell Ackoff, noted strategic planning professor and consultant) involved the entire organization in the strategic plan. At Starbucks, every quarter management stands in front of all employees in open forums everywhere they do business to discuss the last quarter's results. They also discuss openly all plans, decisions, strategies, and concerns. Starbucks' financial performance over a five-year period was at the top of the *Fortune* 1000, both on shareholder returns and cash-flow growth.

The trend is toward involving employees in *all* strategic decisions. It makes sense, since it *is*, after all, everybody's business. It involves their lives. It is appropriate that they be involved. And it makes even more sense given the extraordinary results that come from even partial involvement.

The old saying that corporate management is not a democracy may need to be retired. What's on the table here are results from involvement that are consistently much higher. Thirty to 50 percent gains are common. Job descriptions and performance appraisal can, at best, account for 70 percent of potential performance. You cannot coerce exceptional performance. It requires that employees choose to give their best because it is in their best interests or because it is in the best interests of those the company serves.

The alternative of *not* involving employees in the organization's business offers still more compelling evidence for involving them. When distrust of management and its actions are not surfaced and addressed, employees simply do not try as hard. This often results in an "unexplainable" 20 percent decline in production. Net performance, then, is 50 percent below potential!

The opportunity exists for any leader at any level of any organization to act in a "We the People" manner, to encourage employees to voice their concerns and their ideas. When they do so, when they listen and then lead a process for reaching agreement, powerful things happen. In pioneering organizations, people believe in the plans because they helped create them, and their level of commitment is the secret of the pioneering magic.

THE ORGANIZATION CONVERGENCE & COMMITMENT CHECKLIST

The Organization Convergence & Commitment Checklist presented as an exhibit in this chapter was developed from over 25 years of experience as a consultant to a wide variety of organizations. It was drawn from the confidential interviews of more than a thousand employees, ranging from CEOs to the shop floor. These questions and concerns, echoed in interview after interview, helped me understand why peak organizational performance is difficult to achieve, but also why pioneering organizations are able to achieve miracles. The dramatic breakthroughs created by workers and managers as we surfaced and resolved these intrinsic issues led me to the understanding of pioneering organizations. I am indebted to these workers and managers for their openness, candor, and courage regarding the problems they were experiencing in their organizations, and for the caring and commitment they demonstrated in seeking the way ahead.

The Checklist provides leaders with a comprehensive guide for employee involvement. It is one that mirrors the internal assessment process continuously going on inside employees' minds as they decide whether or not to commit their best to the organization and its plans. This process can be used to align individual dreams and corporate purposes. It can create a convergence of leadership, individualism, and teamwork in service of the organization's greatest hopes. The message of this book has been that when these three forces converge, organizations reach a moment of unified consciousness in which extraordinary things are possible.

Further evidence for the universality of these issues is that most of them have also been partially addressed by many other approaches to performance improvement over the past two decades. Most of those programs, however, covered only one or two of the issues; none addressed all of them. The *Convergence & Commitment Checklist* attempts to be a complete guide. It covers all the issues voiced by actual managers and employees concerning their organizations—strategies, plans, benefits and costs, individual concerns, teamwork and trust concerns, and problems in meetings and work processes.

THE ORGANIZATION CONVERGENCE

ORGANIZATIONAL ISSUES ➡	• Is this a good place to work?

BUSINESS ISSUES Are we doing the right things in the right ways?	INDIVIDUAL ISSUES Can I achieve my goals working here?
S T R A T E G Y •Are we in the right markets with the right customers? •Are we providing the services and products our customers need? •Are we pursuing any pioneering breakthroughs? •Do we have appropriate goals? •Is our human resource strategy on target? •Am I confident in the overall strategy?	•Will the business strategy benefit me? •Will my job be more secure or less? •Will I be doing interesting and important things? •Will there be development opportunities and training?
P L A N N I N G •Do I believe our plans can work? •Do our plans have management support? •Will our systems, policies and procedures help or hinder? •Is there role clarity and buy-in? •Do we have enough people and know how? •Do we have adequate resources? •Which work is value-added, which should be stopped?	•The plan may be good for the business, but will it also benefit me? •Can I make a valued contribution? •To what degree will I be able to plan my own work? •Is individual initiative welcome? •Will my contributions be recognized and rewarded?
E X E C U T I O N •Is everyone executing according to plan? •Are efforts being coordinated? •Is upper management providing sufficient support? •Do we face problems and solve them?	•Is my work going well, or am I frustrated and overwhelmed? •Are my needs and concerns being addressed? •Am I getting the support I need?
E V A L U A T I O N •Are we evaluating the right things? •Do we measure progress toward vision, mission, and goals? •Do we give and get useful feedback? •Are performance evaluations appropriate? •Do we analyze results and learn from them? •Do we normally succeed or fall short?	•Are my efforts recognized and appreciated? •Am I being adequately rewarded now? Will I be in the future? •Am I learning and gaining experience that will advance my career?

AND COMMITMENT CHECKLIST

- Am I proud to be working for this organization? → • Do I trust this organization's leadership?

TEAMWORK ISSUES Can I count on sufficient teamwork?	TRUST ISSUES Can I trust that others will do what is needed?	PROCESS ISSUES Will our meetings, systems, and processes help or hinder?
•Will my peers be supportive of the business strategy or will they resist it? •Does the strategy make good use of our unit's strengths? •Will employment opportunities be expanded or reduced for our group? •Are my interests aligned with the group or different?	•Do I trust management's intentions? Are they serving the interests of all? •Are people saying what they believe about the strategy or what is expected? •Does the strategy build on our core competencies?	•Are we focused on strategy or bogged down in details? •Are we talking about the real issues? •Are people listening and trying to understand all views and values? •Is communication good in all directions?
•Is the plan supported by those who will be involved? •Is everyone committed to doing what it takes? •Are interests sufficiently aligned for good teamwork? •Will management be supportive?	•Do people intend to do what they say they will? •Are they able to do what is needed? •Are there plans to keep everything visible and to hold all accountable? •Will management live up to their commitments?	•Are we competing or collaborating? •Are we able to reach agreements and commit to them? •Is there a sense of synergy or of separateness? •Are meetings good or bad? •Is the planning process sufficient? •Do all units and all levels have a voice in all plans affecting the whole?
•Is our teamwork what it needs to be? In all directions? •Are all plans moving forward? Do we need to adjust roles or assignments? •Is everyone benefiting?	•Are people doing what they committed to? •Are others helping or hindering me in getting my part done? •Is everyone doing a fair share? •Is management living up to their word?	•Are we communicating? •Are people working synergistically or separately? Are efforts aligned up and down the chain of command? •Do we work together to overcome setbacks? •Are systems, policies, and procedures helping or hindering?
•Are appropriate rewards and recognition being provided for all contributions? •Have we gotten together to evaluate the total effort and to learn from it? •Did we get together to celebrate our successes?	•Is there sufficient trust for useful feedback in all directions? •Are evaluation efforts and performance appraisals unbiased? •Are contributions being fairly recognized and rewarded?	•Was this a pleasant or punishing effort? •Did everything flow together smoothly or were there constrictions? •Did all processes work adequately or do some need overhaul?

© Copyright Larry N. Davis 1995-2000

No checklist can ever completely capture the full truth of any complex phenomenon. This one, however, accounts for all of the issues that people were able to report as factors affecting their commitment.

The checklist graphically and sequentially shows how individual choices work for or against commitment and ultimately toward organizational strength or weakness. Consequently, it provides a protocol that leaders can use in creating an open dialogue around relevant issues. Like it or not, employees are instinctively assessing their environment and deciding whether or not to give their all or to hold back. The Checklist provides leaders with an opportunity to influence that decision. It is not about selling and convincing; it is about sharing, listening, and responding. It calls for leaders to interact authentically and openly with employees about what should be done and why, and what the costs and benefits to all might be. The stern message here is that commitment is not achieved by tricks, gimmicks, or inspiring words. It is achieved by surfacing and resolving the doubts and concerns people have, so they will reciprocally commit to serving the organization's goals. There is no other way. The good news however, is that this is also a process and checklist for developing the extraordinary potential I have called pioneering.

Questions Based on Interviews

The questions in the Checklist were initially the concerns voiced by the managers and employees in more than a thousand interviews at all levels in a wide range of organizations. The interviews were held in preparation for performance improvement efforts. They were not my questions. They came in response to general questions, such as "What is helping you and hindering you in doing your job?" That did not mean that each person had all of these questions. In fact, people usually had between six and 10 main concerns. The rest were not issues for them in their organization at that time. Later use of the Checklist, however, indicated that all of the questions were important to a majority of the people interviewed.

The 80-plus questions are not all of the original questions that were raised, but are instead representative forms of all the questions.

In that way, they are like survey items covering every type of topic that was mentioned. The categories of six issues and four stages (discussed below) are my attempt to understand the nature of the concerns and to organize them in a useful fashion. The sequence (again discussed below) does, however, as closely as possible represent the "natural" sequence in which they had to be resolved.

The sequence is indicated by the arrows on the checklist. First, the Organizational Issues must be resolved, then the Business Issues, Individual Issues, etc. The specific questions involved are somewhat different for each stage of the business cycle—strategy, planning, execution, and evaluation. While all of these stages are to some degree present all of the time, managers and employees think in terms of the one that is most in play.

The Six Issues

All of the questions and concerns voiced by managers and employees in the interviews fall into six fundamental issues. They can be summarized by the following questions.

1. Organizational Issues: Is this a good place to work?
2. Business Issues: Are we doing the right things, in the right way?
3. Individual Issues: Can I achieve my goals and meet my needs working here?
4. Teamwork Issues: Can I expect teamwork from all involved?
5. Trust Issues: Can I trust that everyone can and will do what is needed?
6. Process Issues: Will our meetings, systems, and processes help or hinder us?

The Four Stages

In the interviews, there were past, present, and future concerns. As people talked, it was clear that they were describing similar but different things according to whether they were speaking of something in the planning, implementation, or evaluation stage. According to their level in the organizational structure, interviewees were more or less likely to divide concerns into strategic or operational planning issues. Consequently, I employed the four-stage business cycle you see in the Checklist.

As I said earlier, the strategic issues were largely about the organization's strategy, and not everyone had a basis for an opinion. The other three stages are largely from the perspective of the specific division or work unit within the organization.

The Sequence

In the interviews, people raised their concerns in random order, but as I talked with them further, it appeared that they assessed organizations and their work in a particular sequence in making the decision to commit full or minimum effort. As such, this sequence seems to be the psychological sequence of commitment. Let me describe the thought process as I believe it typically occurs.

First people assess the organization and its leadership. If employees have negative feelings about the organization's true mission or distrust the leadership, there will be limited commitment—a "just do the job and draw the paycheck" attitude. If their organizational assessment is positive, the assessment proceeds. The next question in deciding how much to commit is "Are we doing the right things in the right ways for the right reasons?" If the answer is "No," the inquiry is over then and there. A fully committed effort will not occur. If the answer they arrive at is "Yes," then the next question is about their individual purposes and interests.

The individual issue questions take a form like the following: "This may be the best thing for the organization, but is it good for me?" Taken together, the three assessments up to this point are the questions of individualism—service and self-interests. Again, a "No" means the inquiry is over. If the assessment about self-interests yields a "Yes," however, then "Can I expect teamwork from all involved?" comes as the next question. With a "No" here, the situation is more complex. The peer group issues cut both ways. Loyalty to the group may cause employees to hold back, but if they are convinced that the right way has been found and that the peer group will be against it (a situation experienced frequently by individualists), the decision may be to commit and go against the group. This may be the right choice, but it often causes problems in implementation.

Trust now becomes the issue. "Do I trust the other people involved" becomes a crucial question if the answers up to this point have been "Yes" and the employee is ready to fully commit. "Do I believe they can and will do what is needed?" Trust is an issue at all times, but up to this point it was not decisive. If an employee is not putting much into an effort anyway, given other earlier assessments, it really does not make much difference to them whether or not they trust the other people involved. When, however, they are ready to commit and are inclined to go the extra mile, they begin to concern themselves with whether other people truly intend to do what they say and are competent to do what is needed? A "No" about trust means I am likely to protect myself by holding back. A kind of wait-and-watch attitude takes over.

Finally, the process becomes the issue. Employees make an assessment about such things as meetings, systems, procedures, and planning processes. They concern themselves with whether or not these things will support or hinder their work and whether their experience will be positive or negative. No matter how committed they have been up to this point, if the experience is too unpleasant, people will pull back. Many performance improvement programs have tried to start here, working on such things as communication, tolerance of personality and cultural differences, and meeting skills. These are all important, but not sufficient. Consequently, any commitments formed about these tend to break down quickly if a firm foundation of commitment does not exist for all the other issues.

Something close to the above sequence seems to occur for most people in the initial decision to commit. If a "No" resulted in a "just do the job" lack of commitment, the situation is likely to remain that way indefinitely. Employees simply go through the motions and draw a paycheck. People seldom initiate their own reassessments of situations perceived to be negative. If, however, an employee makes a decision to commit, the assessment is often continuous and sometimes tenuous. All of these issues are on the table at all times, and any negatives can cause employees to withdraw or lessen their commitment. Maintaining commitment requires a continuous process of surfacing and addressing issues. That is the job of leaders. The issues do not always have to be resolved as employees would like, but they must be taken seriously and addressed. When they are not, employees simply give up on the place, but often stick around to draw their paychecks.

Leaders can also use this sequence as the most effective one for working toward a convergence of the interests of individuals, the concerns of teams, and organizational goals. They can start by asking people to assess the current state of the organization and the work they are doing and then to envision better ways to do things. They can continue by asking them to candidly discuss their degree of satisfaction in the work they are doing and the degree to which they feel they are able to achieve their own goals. This sets the stage for discussions about teamwork and trust. Finally, leaders should inquire about processes and whether the processes work in maintaining communication and supporting employees in accomplishing organizational and personal goals. At each step, leaders should ask whether employees feel they are getting the management support they need.

This sequence parallels the classical stages of group dynamics—forming, storming, norming, and performing. In that theory, however, the view is usually that groups just have to go *through* these stages. There are few actionable ideas for how to help them. The theory has limits in application to work organizations. The forming stage is really only fully relevant to new teams. In the storming stage, one might do better to pay attention to what they are mostly storming about—what should be done and how to do it. The norming stage concerns reaching agreements about these work issues and the norms of the process of working together. Performing then clearly results from people being committed because they have worked through all of these issues. Why wait for this to happen naturally or maybe not happen at all? It is possible for groups and organizations to move through these stages in a nanosecond given the guidance of someone with a little experience with the sequence and the process.

Other Uses of the Checklist
for Achieving Convergence and Commitment

In conclusion, consider a number of additional ways leaders can use the Checklist, as well as examples of how others have used it. In the next chapter, I will describe in greater depth several ways leaders can specifically deal with each of the six different kinds of issues.

- Leaders can simply use the checklist as a guide in holding spontaneous discussions with employees in meetings or even in hallway conversations. They can ask questions randomly and stay with the thread of discussion, using the Checklist only to assure themselves that everything has been covered.

- Leaders can ask employees a simple, open-ended question, like "What is helping you and hindering you in getting the job done?" They can then refer to the Checklist to ask about any specifics that are not mentioned, often because they are not a problem at that time. Remember, it is as important to find out what is working as it is to find out what is wrong.

- Leaders can simply hand out copies of the Checklist and ask employees to circle the items that are a problem. They can then lead a discussion about the circled items and work with employees to come up with solutions. The Checklist serves well as a quick diagnostic. Employees tend to quickly identify two to three areas that need work and often give an OK to all the rest. In breakdown situations, there will be more issues, but still, the Checklist helps employees quickly target the most important ones. The problem areas are not only different in different organizations and different parts of organizations, but they tend to vary over time, given different priorities and different conditions.

- Finally, leaders can simply use the Checklist to conduct their own quick diagnosis. In my experience, the items they pinpoint when I have initial discussions with them are usually the same ones the employees bring up in meetings or in interviews. Intuitively, the leaders know where the problems are, but many times they have not yet crystallized their thinking. The Checklist helps them be thorough.

An example of a recent use of the Checklist was at Classic Communications, where Kay Monigold, EVP in charge of call centers, held employee involvement sessions in the centers. She used the general "helps/hinders" question and led employees through a process of prioritizing problems and developing proposals and action plans. The Checklist served as a basis for assuring that all possible concerns had been discussed. Interestingly, without having seen the checklist, employees identified one or two issues in each of the six categories, but focused in on three for priority attention. Having discussed them, some of the other items were simply taken care of by the employees themselves within the next few days. Small teams are continuing to follow up on other items. In one of the centers where there had been a history of problems, there is a new sense of teamwork.

The high point came when a woman named Charlie, a staff trainer who had been championing pay classification increases for others' jobs (this was one of the priority discussion items), finally sheepishly raised her hand. "I hate to mention this," she said, "but my kind of job—staff jobs—are not on the list. To be comparable, we really need increases too." Kay thanked her for bringing it up. It was an oversight on everybody's part, and as it turned out there were some problematic inequities there. Normally, employees find it difficult to openly bring up pay issues, and yet their commitment is negatively affected by feelings of unfairness. The fact that Charlie was able to bring it up is a testimony to how comfortable a session can become after a few hours of candid discussion; it is also a testimony to Kay's leadership skills.

CONVERGENCE FOLLOWS VISION

Pioneering vision is the first requirement of a pioneering organization, but a convergence of interests is a close second. With the help of the Checklist, convergence can be achieved in most organizations most of the time, providing that leaders truly believe in serving the interests of all. Almost anything can be done in a way that benefits everyone. In the next chapter, we will consider in depth the six issues and ways to surface them and move toward convergent solutions.

Working Through the Six Key Issues

"**W**e had been bogged down with those problems for so long," said a software engineer with Lockheed at NASA in 1983. "Everyone was mad at everyone else. As we worked through the issues, each time we reached an agreement, the room seemed to rise about six inches. By the time we finished the last item, I felt like saying, 'Houston, we have liftoff!'"

That comment is from memory, and it may not be an exact quote, but it captures the gist of what he said. It is typical of comments that participants make at the end of successful improvement sessions in which they face and work through issues. Guardedness drops away; people relax again; they begin to feel some new enthusiasm for their work, to experience renewed commitment, and their performance usually improves. *The Organization Convergence & Commitment Checklist* (see pages 130-131) can help groups surface and resolve hidden issues. Having individually identified the issues as they see them, the Checklist helps provide a context for the problems they are facing and points them toward solutions.

The questions in the six issue columns essentially speak for themselves. They represent the kinds of concerns voiced repeatedly by managers and employees about their organizations, the work being done in them, and their participation in that work. I'd like to discuss these concerns as a basis for understanding how leaders might help their groups work through them. That way, leaders will have a description of actions they can take to help create a convergence of individualism, teamwork, and leadership in service of the organization's goals.

Leadership fundamentally is about bringing people together to work energetically toward common goals. All of the questions in the Checklist are about those goals, their appropriateness, and the actions needed to accomplish them. They exist as internal assessments that all are making in deciding the degree and quality of their participation. Creating full, open, and thoughtful consideration of these questions is therefore one of the most practical actions that a leader could ever take.

The human tendency, however, is to act like no questions or doubts exist and to urge people into action. Such questions could, after all, delay and deflect current efforts to get the job done. But it is dangerous for leaders to ignore the impact of this natural human process of self-guidance and self-protection, particularly in this age in which instant and abundant information continuously feeds these questions.

To guard against the tendency to push past such questions, I recommend that leaders look inside themselves to notice these same questions and concerns and to reflect on the process they went through to resolve them. It will then become authentic and apparent for leaders to continuously act to surface, address, and resolve as many of these concerns as possible. Also, by sharing their own doubts and their ideas of what to do about doubts, leaders increase their credibility with employees.

These questions should also be useful for organization development professionals. Since organizations are conscious, choice-determinant systems (see Chapter 11), the Checklist can be viewed as a map of employee choice. The questions in the six columns can serve as a reliable checklist of potential employee concerns and as a basis for designing activities that can aid in developing organizations.

Remember that the strategy stage issues in all of the issue columns tend to be about the organization as a whole, while the other three stages are more about specific divisions or units.

A WORD OF CAUTION

Before we proceed with an issue-by-issue analysis, however, a word of caution. The collaborative, non-hierarchical processes being described throughout this book are powerful tools for organizational convergence and performance. They work because they recognize that employees of all levels want their organizations to work. Human beings have always come together through organization to get things done. They know how to do it. They want to do their part, and they want to benefit along with everyone else.

Most people, up and down in every kind of organization, are good business partners with an innate sense for looking at "business realities." They understand the need to provide a good product at a good cost. They know about tight resources. They know how to think about these things, and they want to make sure their actions help the mutual enterprise. They feel it is "their" organization, not so much in the sense of owning it, but in the sense of *being* it. A convergence of interests is possible because it is natural, and given half a chance, people will choose it. The power struggle can end now. It is time.

All of us, however, have some broken parts. We react to situations from inner needs that are not clear to us and cannot be satisfied in ways appropriate to the situation. We make it difficult for others. But if given a chance, most of us can eventually work things out with others through such processes; and the truth is, we want to.

A few people, however, are unable to do this. They have lifelong problems with authority—anybody's authority—and they have trouble working with others and being committed to anything. These processes will not work for them. When as a leader you have made a good effort at working things through, and there is still someone who will not agree to anything and cannot be satisfied, thank them for their participation, treat them with respect, but stop trying to satisfy them. Focusing on them becomes a disservice to everyone else. As soon as possible, separate them from such group activities and deal with their concerns through more traditional HR means. Fortunately, they are few in number—a very small percentage. Most of us are just ornery some of the time, and it takes a few rounds for us to work it through. Those who can't work things through, however, if not dealt with, can harm these processes and the organization.

THE ORGANIZATION ISSUES

The issues concerning pride in the organization and trust in top management color everything employees do. Consequently, managers who would like to move their organizations to the extraordinary levels of pioneering organizations must concern themselves with these fundamental employee assessments. When there are negative assessments, these issues are relatively difficult matters to address. To do so, leaders must become involved with employees of all levels in creating an organization for which everyone can feel pride.

The first concern that must be addressed is the degree with which employees identify with the purposes of the organization— their pride or lack of pride in the products and services provided by the organization, their commitment to its vision. Typically, many employees are indifferent, and indifferent employees do not show the commitment of going the extra mile. But why are they indifferent? It is a leader's job to find out why and to turn those attitudes around. Every employee's belief in what he or she is helping to provide goes to the heart of customer service. Leadership consequently requires an ongoing and open assessment of the company's value to customers and community.

Here is one case in point. I was privileged to hear many exchanges over a period of 10 years between Don Buchanan, a senior plant manager at Pendleton Woolen Mills, and all levels of employees and managers at the company about the quality of their products. He was never satisfied, but his comments did not berate the employees. Instead, he engaged them in discussions about making better shirts and blankets. He made it clear to everyone that those products were intended to last a lifetime. The pride of the Mill workers in Pendleton and in Portland was evident. It was shared by the residents of Oregon. And it is shared by most people who have ever owned Pendleton clothing or blankets.

Beyond the organization's products and services, corporate citizenship also impacts employee pride in the organization. Even though employees often publicly defend their organization when it is charged with ecological or customer harm—their salaries often depend on their organization's not being convicted—such negatives seem to affect morale and performance. A cynical mood prevails, and performance shows signs of low commitment.

The second issue concerns trust in the organization's leadership. In recent years, distrust has become far more common than in previous decades. That distrust usually concerns "downsizing" and the many reported instances of employee layoffs accompanied by large increases in top management compensation. Beyond this resentment, there are other kinds of damage that come from downsizing. One of them identified in an IBM study and in studies of other corporate downsizing programs is a form of "survivor syndrome" guilt. The more common damage, however, is a lingering insecurity—an "it could happen to me next" attitude. Despite some management beliefs to the contrary, insecurity is not very "motivational."

This erosion of trust in management should be of great concern. While it apparently has not affected productivity, there may yet be a price to pay. Major strikes in the summer of 1998 may be a signal of things to come. I am not recommending rewarding workers for unproductive work; and I am certainly not recommending rewarding them by giving in to entitlement concepts like being paid "to go home when you've done your quota," particularly when better mechanization and systems account for a great deal of the gain in productivity—not faster, more efficient work by the employees. But I also do not recommend that managers be bonused for artificial, short-term profits. As I said earlier in the book, compensation without contribution is theft.

Those leaders who want to enjoy employee trust will need to see their role as serving the best interests of all, not just the stockholders. The principles for convergent leadership outlined in Chapters 3 and 6 serve as a guide.

THE BUSINESS ISSUES

The first and most important lesson for leaders is that it is everybody's business. The traditional "hired hand" concept of employees will no longer serve. The situation is "pay me now, or pay me later." If you do not involve employees up front in all the business issues that affect them, they will involve themselves later through their instinctive assessments, and the results are frequently negative.

Most organizations today involve employees in the planning, implementation, and evaluation of the work performed in their areas. The added value of tapping their highly relevant competence has become obvious. What I am advocating is involving employees continuously in the strategic business issues (see Chapter 12 for methods). The decisions made there affect job security and trust in management. By being involved in deliberations concerning major business challenges, employees gain the opportunity to affect their own destinies. This is the call to individualism and entrepreneurship. It also creates the sense of belonging and making a difference in achieving shared goals that helps build a pioneering spirit.

Not long ago, I had the opportunity to sit in on a meeting of Dell managers and employees who were charged with the responsibility for worldwide procurement. Procurement and supply-chain management are major pieces in the overall Dell strategy. The group was trying to deal with some major challenges resulting from instability in the global economy. In attempting to find solutions to the procurement problem, they were not limiting their thinking to meeting their goals for that year. Instead, they were getting excited by a search for ways to take advantage of the crisis by structuring a whole new strategy. They did not just want to do what was expected of them. They wanted to do the miraculous. They were armed and motivated in this search by information that went far beyond their units goals in meeting profit targets. They were aided by the top-level strategic analysis of profit strategy. They could clearly see how doing better—a lot better—than their goal would boost profits and increase the value of their stock. This Dell philosophy has produced a bumper crop of young millionaires.

The questions in the business issues column are mostly about the degree of confidence in the strategy, plans, execution, or evaluation. People often have very different ideas about what should be done and how it should be done. Typically, if it is not done their way, they do not believe it will work. When they do not believe it will work, they do not give it their best effort. A high percentage of the conflicts, disagreement, and misalignment in organizations are of this type, not personality conflicts. Consequently, good business results depend on surfacing and resolving these differences, to say nothing of the value of the great new ideas that employees will contribute in the process.

This is leadership where it counts—in the thick of things. Not lost in the pixel dust of computer screens. Not locked up in boardrooms. Not issuing inspiring platitudes. But right in the middle of discussions involving all affected parties in addressing and resolving these differences. Addressing the issues is the first important thing. And the second is not covering them up with business-as-usual Band-Aids where the uncleaned wounds fester. What is needed is working *with* employees for solutions, not trying to second-guess them. "It's the discussion, stupid," one wants to say. That's the forum in which a sense of belonging is developed, good ideas emerge, agreements are made, and commitment takes place. No extra cost.

Merritt Belisle, CEO of Classic Communications, tells a story about his big lesson in employee involvement. He was having his first meeting with the employees of a rural cable company he had just acquired. He had told them about all of the benefits and what the new company was doing for them. He thought it was a pretty good deal and that they would be pleased, but there was little reaction in the room.

So on an impulse, he said, "Do you have any suggestions for me?" After a moment, a young woman in the back of the room raised her hand. She identified herself as a customer service rep who took incoming calls (the lowest paid position in the company). "I was wondering if we could buy an ad in the Feist Area Wide Guide (a regional rural telephone directory), advertising our 800 number," she said. "People don't know it. In some of those small towns where we don't have a local office, people are having to chase down our trucks to get the number. I think it's hurting business. I told the manager before you, but he said the ad would cost too much. So I wanted to ask you."

Merritt was stunned. Given the silence, he had expected complaints about the salaries or benefits. But given the opportunity to talk about anything, here was this employee talking about the business and about good customer service. "Yes, we can buy the ad," he said. "I'll do it tomorrow." Apparently, this broke the ice because after the meeting, several of the techs came up and told him about some problems with their trucks that were getting in the way of their doing a good job. And so it went. That little group of employees in Plainville, Kansas, performed so well that he put his call center there, making them the hub of operations for a multi-state area. They do great customer phone calls there.

"I decided at that moment," Belisle says, "that I would create an organization in which people could question whether or not the emperor had on any clothes." His decision has paid off. Classic Communications has been able to figure out how to bring full service cable to rural areas that no one believed could be profitable. Classic Communications is now the 13th largest cable provider in the United States and still growing.

The good news is that employees care about the business. And the other good news is that business issues are subject to rational debate and logic. When people have trouble coming to agreement after a lot of discussion, they are usually willing to experiment, to try something out and see what works, and then go with that. Consensus is ideal, but most employees are willing to support whatever is decided after a full hearing of their ideas.

THE INDIVIDUAL ISSUES

"The plan may be good for the organization, but is it good for me?" emerges as the most important question at this point. Self-interest is not only natural, but it is also useful. It is the basis for all human motivation. It should certainly not be treated as a form of unworthy selfishness. Selfishness has to do with not sharing. Self-interest is the authentic foundation for sharing. Self-interests are not antithetical to service; they are a natural and healthy basis for it. Individualism is an integration of the two. Aligned self-interest is also a solid way to build teamwork. Furthermore, enlightened self-interest is not just a good principle to guide entrepreneurial activity and ownership; it is right for workers too. It should be a guiding principle for an emerging age of economic democracy.

We can believe that the strategy and plan are on target, perhaps even the best possible ones for the organization, but still not be motivated to give them our best. A senior partner at Booz·Allen & Hamilton made this very clear one day. Just after he and his partners had reached consensus on a strategy and plan for their division—one they had labored over for four long days—he remarked almost as an aside that he thought it was right for the firm, but not particularly good for him. The air of celebration went out of the room. He was asked to explain the remark. "Since I'm retiring next year, as everyone knows," he said, "I've given a lot of thought to what I want to do next. The plan, while a good one, and I voted for it, does not provide a means for me to develop in the direction of my new interests." It took only 20 minutes for the group to adjust the plan so that he could develop those interests. Not only were the adjusted strategy and plan successful, but that senior partner created the most business, revenue, and profit for the group that year—his last year in the firm.

THE TEAMWORK ISSUES

There is a built-in conflict in teamwork. People naturally want to belong and have an instinct toward loyalty, but they also want to do what they think is right. This can create a conflict between individuals and their units. It happens frequently when people serve on cross-functional projects. There can also be a conflict between self-interests and peer-group interests.

Leaders, particularly when they are employing cross-functional project teams, need to be particularly aware of this conflict potential. Cross-functional planning is of course a valuable practice, but this conflict limits planning effectiveness in ways that are frequently not recognized. There is too often an assumption that the representative from a group can somehow deliver that group's support for the cross-functional plan. More frequently, however, there is too little sensitivity to the *internal conflict* participants experience. Their loyalty to their peer group and sometimes their fear of being seen as a turncoat or a sellout can seriously constrain the options considered by a cross-functional team. Leaders can guard against these potential problems by openly discussing them, describing their own mixed loyalties, and encouraging others to describe their experiences.

The mixed loyalty problem cropped up a few years ago at Abbott Labs in a cross-functional effort to increase production on one of their lines. The cross-functional team was made up of mechanics, operators, and engineers. Initially, everyone was blaming everyone else. "You can never find a mechanic when you need one," the operators complained. "They won't shut down the machines long enough to give us an opportunity to fix them right," the mechanics countered. "Everyone, both mechanics and operators, is adjusting the machines differently," the engineers chimed in. "How can we tell what needs to be reengineered?"

It took a lot of talk and a lot of facilitation, but finally members of the group were beginning to admit that some of the people in their function were guilty of the behaviors being alleged by the other groups. You could see them looking around nervously as they admitted this, wondering if their disloyalty would be reported to their peers back on the floor. This, however, was the moment of breakthrough. Once the protective façade was dropped, the group quickly developed a tag-team partnering structure for their line that they believed would maximize teamwork and production.

They knew these ideas would not be popular, but they made a commitment to go out of that room as one voice and to sell the plan to their respective peer groups. They sealed this commitment when each of them stepped forth and signed the plan, "just like they did the Declaration of Independence," one of them observed. Initially, there was a lot of resistance, but their commitment carried them through. It was decided to try the plan for a week. The results were staggering. Production shot up. Morale and working conditions vastly improved. Harmony replaced bickering. And these traitors were now heroes.

Teamwork works, but it takes individualistic courage. My advice to leaders is to avoid the recent fads about teams that tend to suppress individualism. Both the language and concept of being a team player is part of the problem. The categorizing of people into personality types who either tend toward teamwork or resist it makes matters worse. A misuse of the word *consensus* has also played a role. Its proper use is to *align committed action*. It was never meant to suppress argument or disagreement, but unfortunately that has become something of a norm. Consensus should be what emerges *after the argument*. David McCabe, an EVP at Classic Communications put it this way, "let's not let consensus overwhelm conviction." Using consensus to avoid conflict creates agreements that result in lukewarm commitment. When no conflict arises, it can mean that no one cares enough and there is little commitment. Facing conflict and resolving it provides the energy for extraordinary action.

THE TRUST ISSUES

"Can I trust the other people?" "Do I believe that they mean what they say?" "Are we communicating honestly?" "Can I count on them?" "Are they willing and able to do what is needed?" These are some of the ways that people phrase their questions about trust. Trust can be defined as a readiness for unguarded interaction with someone or something.[10] If I do not trust the other people who will be involved, I will be cautious and hold myself back as a means of protection. This is one of the most common constraints on committed action.

151

Trust issues can be explosive, but much of the time they are not verbalized. They stay inside, quietly constricting the lifeblood and energy that are needed to achieve the organization's goals. Low trust could be called the silent killer. Trust problems are based on our perceptions of each other's intentions and abilities. We question whether others are willing and able to do what is needed.

Since trust issues are based on perceptions, arguments based on "facts" will often make matters worse. What helps most is for leaders to initiate a process that assures that those involved first reach agreement on "what is needed." Many trust problems arise from having differing expectations about what needs to happen. The cure is effective communication about expectations.

For example, a group of partners in a large international consulting firm were embroiled in a feud that had been going on for a few years. Two of the senior partners, one from New York and one from Chicago, were accusing each other of incompetence on one hand and sabotage on the other. Each had gone to grievance committees and to the board. They would not talk to each other directly. The other partners had geographically taken sides. Business was suffering.

Senior management finally intervened and told them to settle it or leave. And so they met with their partners to do so. It was tough going at first, but finally the group was able to settle down to a rational examination of what was really needed to make the business work. As it turned out, each of these senior partners had been partially right and partially wrong. But it became very clear that they had not agreed on what was needed, and that was the problem, not sabotage or incompetence. With this agreement in place, the partners were able to apologize to each other and admit their errors. They formed a committed partnership. Within a few months, their business was flourishing again. And perhaps more important, people were smiling again as they came to work.

Beyond agreeing on what is needed, processes that help build trust must afford sufficient safety for those involved to self-declare any limits on their intentions (e.g., conflicting priorities that could lead to their doing less than they intend or less than is called for by the work).

It should also be comfortable to voice any doubts they may have about their own ability to do what is needed. "I'm really good at this part," a top manager used to say, "but I don't have a clue about that other matter. Does anybody else here have an idea?" Admitting what we don't know or can't do is one of the hardest things for human beings. Comments like this by leaders make it easier.

Once people have authentically critiqued themselves, it then becomes far less threatening for others to express any additional concerns they may have. Such a process can lead to tangible trust agreements and more trustworthy expectations.

THE PROCESS ISSUES

These issues are about the experience of working together. We may have trouble understanding someone or feel like they do not understand us. We may experience the meetings we attend as being efficient and effective or dull and draining. We may find working together to be a pleasant or a punishing experience. The procedures and systems involved in working together may be real killers.

These are the issues that stimulated an avalanche of training over the last two decades—communication training, personality training and type casting, training in meeting techniques, and systems work. Most of this training can be helpful, but it is not sufficient to produce the kinds of results expected of it. The issues identified in the other five columns of the Checklist must be resolved as well.

Nonetheless, it is important that meeting processes and other processes for working together be experienced as not too unpleasant. When they are too unpleasant, people will avoid them no matter how committed they are in other respects. Many managers who are committed to teamwork across their organizations become so resistant to all of the meetings it seems to require that they stop coming, and teamwork suffers. This is what I call "meeting sickness." It is not just a matter of improving the meetings. We must stop some of them. Meetings have made teamwork seem like a punishment. There are many ways to strengthen teamwork in the middle of the action, and many of them are more fun than meetings.

Process issues are the easiest issues to deal with. People do not tend to take a critique of them personally. Leaders should simply insure that all involved take some time to plan their processes for meeting and working together. Once they take the time to think about it, most groups can design processes that work just right for their needs and tastes.

The systems issues, on the other hand, frequently extend over a broader segment of the organization, and leaders need to take charge of those issues, clearing a path when necessary. Difficult administrative systems can be just as deadly as inefficient manufacturing systems. For instance, at the Austin-Travis County MHMR, the counselors were not implementing some new family therapy practices the agency had spent a bundle on. Was this resistance to change? No, it was due to the fact that three times the amount of paperwork was required to implement the training, and this drastically cut into the already scarce time the counselors had for their case loads. A simple policy and procedure change solved the matter.

A FINAL WORD ON THE CHECKLIST

The Organization Convergence & Commitment Checklist provides leaders and OD professionals with a comprehensive guide to the factors involved in employee commitment. Securing that commitment should be the first order of business for leaders. Doing that and developing organizations to their highest potential requires a convergence of interests. The Checklist provides a means for aligning individual interests, group interests, and the organization's goals. It is a protocol that leaders can use for initiating an open dialogue around these most relevant of issues.

Maintaining convergence and commitment requires a continuous process of surfacing, addressing, and resolving these issues. This is a much richer agenda than the limited technical issues covered by TQM. It reaches to people's souls and the souls of their organizations.

As one final illustration, listen to the words of Charlene, an employee at a Whole Foods Market in Austin. I had asked a sacker if it was a good place to work. His answer was positive, but a little vague. When he had walked away, the checker, whom I had not asked, but who had overheard my question, volunteered an answer that would seem to indicate that for her at least, the leaders had created just such a convergence. She said, "What makes this a good place to work is that there is always something to learn, about our food or the business, and they give you the chance to learn it. And of course the stock and the profit sharing." She went on to tell me that she had worked in some other more traditional food store chains, and that it was not like that in them. Then I asked her about the managers. She gave me a significant look. "Well, they are not like those others in those other stores," she said. "The managers here get down in the trenches with you."

Building
Communication
and Trust

"**O**ur main problem is communication." That is the universal answer to some of the most frequently asked questions. "What's going wrong here? What are the problems? What will it take to move the project forward?" If as a species, we self-destruct, that should be the epitaph on our cosmic tombstone. Human beings must communicate. They are not self-sufficient. They must work together. To accomplish anything complex, they form organizations that enable them to work together effectively. Communication is the most fundamental requirement for organization. When things become routine, the importance of communication can lessen, but when anything changes, communication is essential again. In most organizations today, change is rampant. For pioneering organizations, the mission is change. Communication is crucial.

A pioneering vision propels an organization only if it is known. Convergence is possible only if people talk about and agree to the ways they must work together to reach the goal—who must do what, and who needs what help. Committed convergence can only be achieved if people are able to express and listen to individual desires and needs. In organizations where people cannot talk about their doubts and concerns, catastrophes occur. If managers and employees do not feel free to say they don't know something, can't

157

do it, or feel wrong about doing it, failure is likely and trust will be broken. If communication is not complete and truthful, projects will flounder. Communication will be truthful only when there is a great deal of individual courage or a great deal of trust. Organizations work best when there is both. Pioneering organizations require both.

For about 20 years now, a great many consultants and managers have been exhorting the people in organizations to communicate— to listen well and to speak clearly and to the point. They have also been preaching the importance of trust.

Somehow, people are not getting it. Organizational leaders need to try something different. First, they need to stop preaching and exhorting people to do the obvious. There is a lot of evidence that people in organizations want to communicate better, and that they would if they really knew how. They understand the importance. Somehow, the principles and practices that are being taught must not be right, or if some of them are right, they must not be enough or they may be too simplistic. Maybe what organizational leaders really need to do is to give people in organizations a better understanding of both communication and trust, a list of their separate components, and a simple, step-by-step process for building both— and then trust them to do what is needed.

That is the purpose of this chapter. It provides a clear and comprehensive guide for both communication and trust (tested practical concepts appropriate to organizational settings rather than therapy groups), a list of their separate components, and step-by-step processes for putting them to good use. That's when the leader's job takes over. It is up to you and the other leaders in your organization to make the tools available to everyone working with you, and then you must take the lead in putting the tools to widespread use. Put them out on the walls and on the Web. Hold training sessions. And most important, demonstrate them in all you do in the organization.

That is the action plan for building a culture of communication and trust. Both of these are basic to every interaction in organizations today: they impact everything. And they are the foundation that must exist for you to effectively implement other strategies and practices. They are also the foundation for building a pioneering organization.

COMMUNICATION

Working together in organizations requires communication. It always has, but at earlier stages of human history effective teamwork was just as much about synchronization of effort and physical motion. In today's work settings, most teamwork is mental rather than physical. The action may be fast and furious, but we are passing around ideas not balls, bolts, or boxes. This makes communication the most important action, not physical coordination. It is our mouth and ears that must be most skilled, and the mind that connects them—not our hands, arms, and legs. It is the communication processes involved in teamwork that make the most difference, not techniques or engineering protocols. Clearly then, for organizations to be effective, people need to learn the basic principles of effective communication; they need to practice regularly; they need to put the communication practices into play; and they need to "review the game films" to see how they did.

The Basics

The basics may seem beneath you, but most people do not truly know them, and that causes most of the problems. Furthermore, much of the material presented here will be new to most; it is not a rehash of the typical communication training that has been around for the last 20 years. Much of that was built on concepts arising from group therapy, personality theory, cognitive styles, or social movements. The concepts presented here were developed in organizational settings and have been tested under fire.

Let's start by defining and describing communication because it can mean a lot of different things to different people. In fact, that is what creates many of the problems. One person's "communication" does not communicate to the other—often because of an incomplete understanding of communication. Here's a definition that will help.

While it was developed in working with organizations and teams, it is also compatible with certain academic communication theories.

Communication is a process of exchange in which people use signals to attempt to gain the cooperation of others in doing what they think needs to be done.[11]

Let's take that one line at a time.

Communication is a process of exchange . . .

First, communication is a process. It is not an event, and it is not a one-liner, such as a statement of fact or a sound byte of information. These may be *what* someone is attempting to communicate— the content of the communication—but the mere existence of data in the air or on paper does not make communication. Information must be *received* for a communication to exist, and some would say it must be understood. So we can say this process has in it two primary actions: sending (a signal or message) and receiving. That's where most communication theory stops, but that is not the end of the story. Communication is a process of exchange. Generally, when we give something in an exchange, we expect to get something in return; we expect a *response*. When something is only sent and received, it is more like a gift than an exchange. But we'll get to that in a moment.

Now, let's look at the second part of the definition.

. . . in which people use signals . . .

The word *signals* is used rather than *messages* because it conveys a wide range of human expression beyond language, which covers a relatively narrow band of the full range of communicative behavior (but in the text, signals and messages will be used interchangeably). By this advanced age, we are all aware of nonverbal communication and its importance (not so 30 years ago), but communication includes even more than these two. Everything said and done can be considered communication if we intend for someone to receive a message. This can, for example, include such things as words, movements, facial expressions, memos, and e-mails, to name some of the more common forms. But communication can also take the form of actions, such as promotions, demotions, or failing to give a raise or bonus, when we want "to send a message." User-friendly and user-abuser procedures or systems can also be said to "communicate an attitude" to employees or customers. Communication can even include things unsaid and undone when silence or inaction express our thoughts or feelings about a matter; we often speak of "letting our actions speak for us" in this manner.

The fact that communication is a process of sending *and receiving* may make the definition even broader. It could make sense, for example, to include all the signals people *think* they receive. Communication would then include everything said and done and everything unsaid and undone that a "receiver" believes was intended for him or her. To define it more narrowly would be to leave unmentioned many of the causes of communication problems—the unintended slights and insults people perceive were meant for them.

This brings us to the third part of the definition.

. . . *to attempt to gain the cooperation of others* . . .

I told you that when we give something in an exchange, we usually intend to get something in return. This is it. We are trying to gain someone's cooperation. We are attempting to get others to help us, or at least not hinder us or harm us. This is the purpose of communication. Even when we are only giving information (FYI), we think the other person may someday use it beneficially, and therefore we expect them to return the favor when appropriate.

The concept that communication has the purpose of gaining cooperation is the unique and definitive feature of this theory and is the reason it is so well suited to organizational work settings. There is no such thing as aimless chatter. When we communicate, we are always after some form of cooperation. And when we don't get it, a communication problem has arisen. Let me clarify the word *cooperation*. We want people to do what we want them to do. The word *compliance* could also, therefore, be read in, but when it is, we've got a problem from the get-go. As I hope you are beginning to see, this stuff called communication is loaded. And today, it is the primary tool of teamwork and organizations!

Finally, let's consider the last part of the definition.

. . . in doing what they think needs to be done.

We expect some form of action. We expect others to *do* something. It may be something verbal, like providing us with information or an apology, or it may be something like completing a project or closing the office door—but it is an action. It is not just a "thank you for sharing." That's why it can sometimes be infuriating when someone only does reflective Rogerian listening (just repeating what we say). Yes, this can feel good up to a point; we feel they are listening, giving us attention, trying to understand us. But unless we specified that listening is all we wanted, when that is *all* they do we start to get irritated at their unresponsiveness. We were, after all, making these noises on purpose; we were not just flapping our gums, we wanted to get them to cooperate in doing what we think needs to be done. And there's the rub. They often have a different view of what needs to be done. That is why trust in organizations starts with a mutual understanding and agreement about what is needed.

Again, the concept that communication is needs-meeting behavior is unique to this theory. You can see why it is so applicable to the quandaries you experience when you go to work each day. It might help you at home too.

From this definition, we can see why communication is the most important action in teamwork. Communication is so pervasive and fundamental to everything that goes on in organizations that it becomes clear why blockages—like the withholding of information, undiscussible subjects, or reticence—breaks down teamwork.

A good example of a communication blockage occurred a few years back in one of the management teams at Booz·Allen & Hamilton. The group had been working for a couple of days to develop a strategic plan for their market segment. They had reached agreement on most of the strategic elements—product offering, pricing, personnel, compensation, and client selection. They had also adopted a number of action plans. Things were moving along well. They should have been feeling good. They did not seem to be.

I stopped their discussion and observed that there was no energy in the room. They agreed. I asked them if they knew why. For a few minutes there was silence. Finally, one of the partners spoke. "To tell you the truth," he said, "I'm scared. Let me tell you what scares me." He went on to comment on their new product offering and client priorities. It was as if a dam broke. Suddenly, everyone was expressing fears. Even though their new strategy was logical, it was not the kind of work most of them valued, and many feared they would not do it well. Others expressed other fears. They made a list. Considering the list of fears, they then changed their plan to be one they could believe in, and in a very short time they created brilliant new strategies. There was excitement in the room and an eagerness to go out and do it. They were very successful that year.

In many organizations, fears are undiscussible. It's a common situation. What was uncommon at Booz · Allen & Hamilton was the partner's courage in describing his fears. This gave new permission and created a new norm for the group. Removing this one communication blockage opened their communication in other ways as well. They spoke with less reserve. Their listening was not only more respectful, it was eager and friendly. They had developed the kind of communication that typifies pioneering organizations.

The Process and the Steps

Definitions are helpful, but for a clearer picture, let's try to see the communication process in motion. The following figure eight diagram depicts that motion.

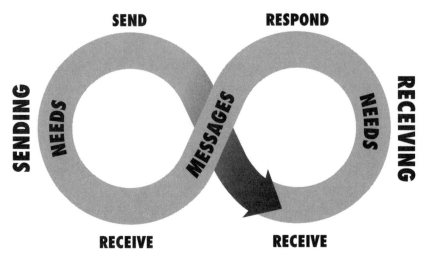

SEND   RESPOND

SENDING   NEEDS   MESSAGES   NEEDS   RECEIVING

RECEIVE   RECEIVE

As you can see from the diagram, a communication exchange involves sending, receiving, and responding. This depicts a two-person communication. In organizations, communication exchanges often involve several people, in which case there is one initial signal sender, all other parties receive, and some respond.

The person who initiates the communication has an initial need in mind (either consciously or unconsciously) and is seeking the cooperation of others in meeting it. In choosing to pay attention, the people who receive the message usually add their own perception of needs to the exchange, either consciously or unconsciously. In most communications, sending and receiving behaviors become essentially simultaneous and reciprocal.

The process becomes more complex when a single one-message communication exchange (the initial point and the responses) develops into a conversation, and both parties are senders *and* receivers of messages. This pattern, depicted by the continuous flow of the arrows, makes it clear that it is important for the needs perceived by all parties to be identified and that a response to everyone's needs is expected. When communication is progressing effectively, this pattern continues until it reaches its intended result—the desired cooperation is agreed to or it is not. That completes the communication. When an agreement to cooperate is the outcome, it sets the stage for further good communication. When it is not, the quality of future communication can decline. Seeing it this way, the process looks more like a form of double helix.

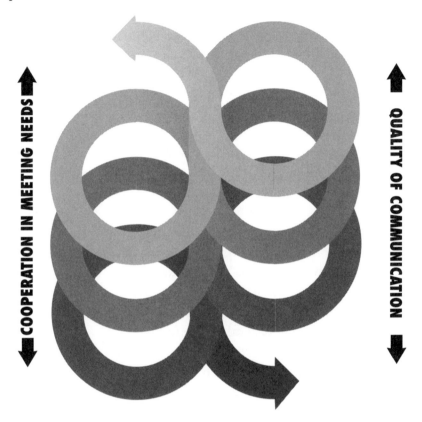

For communication to be successful, three steps must be completed by all parties.

1. *Connection*. Senders must first attempt to get the attention of their intended audience. Timing and courtesy are important here. Receivers must choose to give their full attention and to let that be apparent. A good connection must be made.

2. *Understanding*. Senders must do what it takes to make their message understood. They should make their perception of needs explicit, their purpose clear, their evidence sufficient, the relevance of the message to the other person apparent, and be

prepared to expand and elaborate if requested. Receivers must do what it takes to understand. Both parties are responsible for seeing to it that the exchange of information is sufficient to enable a decision about the desired cooperation.

3. *Response.* Receivers must give a clear response. "Yes," "no," or "I'll have to think about it" are all acceptable responses, providing that in the latter case a time is set for a definitive response. Effective communication is brought to closure by a response and an acknowledgement to that response. Senders are responsible for making sure a response is given, for checking out their own understanding of the response, and for confirming the response. A thank-you helps, no matter the response. Communication is like a proposal. Its successful completion is a decision. A "yes" is of course desired, but a clear and courteous "no" is far better than no response. If the response is too often "no," however, it will erode trust. Trust is better maintained when the receiving party follows a "no" by asking if there is another way to help.

Given the complexity indicated by the figure eight, the double helix, and the steps, it is more incomprehensible that communication succeeds than that so many communication problems arise. The process is even more complex with the instantaneous giving and receiving that occurs in most group communication. It should be clear why mutual identification of needs is so crucial and why it is the single most important key to effective communication.

Since they have received so much attention in recent years, some other views of the communication process need to be mentioned. Much has been made of communication styles (e.g., Myers-Briggs, Neuro-Linguistic Programming, gender differences). Clearly, such styles exist, and it is useful to make a brief study of them and how they result in differences in the ways people communicate. Beyond that, however, their usefulness is questionable. We must still make connection, clarify needs and evidence, and reach a responsive closure. In other words, we are responsible to complete the steps of the communication process described above if we expect good communication. Our willingness to do what it takes to accomplish that is the key. Hiding behind our differences is an excuse.

Furthermore, attempting to remember the different styles and exactly who communicates in what way and how to therefore modify your message, listening, and response to match the other person's is too much ado about too little, and well nigh impossible to boot. This is really apparent in very diverse groups. You simply cannot remember it all in the midst of real conversations and discussions while at the same time tending to the substance, the need-meeting purpose of the communication. Openness and tolerance will go a lot further. The recent fascinations about generalized personality/mind types have become, we might say, a classic example of style without sufficient substance.

On the other hand, at the Post Ranch Inn, they have dealt with an important difference. They provide all employees with Spanish-to-English *and* English-to-Spanish classes. That way, everyone is equally responsible for improving communication.

So far, we have focused primarily on the requirements for effective communication. But communication is not enough. It must be truthful and complete communication. For that, trust is required.

TRUST

We talk a lot about trust. It is a daily concern. When we say we had a good day, chances are we experienced the good, easy energy that flows through us when we feel trusting. When we feel caution or distrust, it is just the opposite. We may experience a tightening, a constricting of energy, or we may feel our energy drop. Sometimes, if our distrust is strong enough, we experience an adrenaline surge of fear and want to run or fight. We typically refer to these as bad days.

We talk a lot about trust, but have not known much about it. What we are experts in is distrust. Trust is one of two natural states that regulate the energy we have available for action and interaction. It is our base state—free-flowing, happy, interactive energy. Its opposite is fear and the various degrees of the chemistry of fear—caution, guardedness, mistrust, distrust, fright, anger, terror, rage. Fear is also a natural state that regulates the energy available for action and interaction. It prepares us for fight, flight, or freeze. The adrenaline chemistry of fear attempts to marshal our energy for protection and defense or for aggression and attack.

Both trust and fear are necessary for survival. But trust is the necessary condition for energetic teamwork between human beings. As such, it is the oxygen for organizational effectiveness. Fear, for the most part, constricts the energy needed for effectiveness or misdirects it in destructive ways. To be sure, in times of crises and external danger, fear or anger can produce a surge of energy that galvanizes a team or an organization into extraordinarily effective action, but these battle conditions are not the daily reality of most groups and organizations. When misguided managers try to make crisis the daily reality, a team's energy will either be badly depleted or the adrenaline energy will be turned inward producing nasty conflicts within the team. Trust is one of the necessary conditions for commitment. Together, commitment and trust build organizational energy. High trust in an organization generally leads to organizational effectiveness; a lack of trust limits it.

To know how to build and maintain trust, leaders need a full understanding of it.

What is Trust?

First, a definition.

Trust is a state of readiness for unguarded interaction with someone or something.[12]

Let's take that one element at a time.

"A state of readiness"

This refers to a psychological state—an attitude. This psychological state is induced by our perceptions of situations in which we find ourselves. Two kinds of perceptions come into play: our perceptions of the *intentions* and our perceptions of the *competence* of others—whether we perceive they are *willing* and *able* to do what is needed. Our perceptions of intentions include such things as whether the other person truly intends to do what seems necessary under the circumstances, or at a more basic level, whether we perceive that their intentions are to help, hinder, or harm us. Our perceptions of competence have to do with whether or not the other person has the knowledge and skills needed to do what is necessary. We may believe that someone has good intentions, but still not want to go mountain climbing with them.

"Unguarded interaction"
This means that the psychological state of readiness has enabled a physical-chemical condition in our bodies that allows our energy to flow freely, unrestrained by caution or fear. We let ourselves go. We freely interact in the situation. We turn our energies to the task at hand.

"With someone or something."
Trust is normally associated with interactions between ourselves and others, but we also experience this attitude in relation to objects such as chairs, computers, and the cosmos. Trust is the essential ingredient for *any* kind of interaction. It is a requirement for successful relationships, teams, marriages, families, organizations, communities, and societies. Trust is the oxygen that enables life beyond mere existence. It liberates the energy of effectiveness.

So Little Trust
It becomes obvious how important trust is to effective organizations. But just how well do we do in building trust and maintaining it? Far too often our efforts could be characterized as "so little trust, so much to do."

This is how our unconscious trust determination usually goes. Our trust, or lack of it, will be determined by our perceptions of intentions and competence. We make judgments about the other person's willingness and ability to do what is needed—as we see it. They make judgments about our willingness and ability—our intentions and competence.

Intentions

Most of us most of the time believe that we
- are willing to do what is needed, and
- generally intend to be helpful.

We question whether the other person is willing to do what's needed, willing to be helpful. We make up reasons for what we hear them say or see them do, and for what they don't say and do. We attribute motives to their actions and inactions. They do the same to us.

Competence

We question other people's competence and try to conceal our own inadequacies. When the ball is dropped, we write people off as incompetent or question their intelligence. Too seldom do we consider that a lack of time may have been the problem; too seldom do we consider that adequate training may not have been available. They do the same to us.

This is the way it usually goes. Without help and a lot of work, most of us do not know much about how to build trust and to maintain it.

Building Trust

What can we do to break this instinctive pattern and consciously build trust? We can work to break the habit of unconscious, instinctive trust/fear judgments—we can try to become conscious of what is blocking our trust. And then we must courageously and caringly share what we find out about our fears with others—with those we want to work closely with and with those with whom we want to be intimate, with our colleagues and our partners.

This is not a matter for games. While "ropes courses" and Outward Bound have some beneficial effects, the trust they produce is temporary and is limited primarily to trust in our teammates' competence. These programs/exercises do little to establish trust in intentions—few of us really believe that our teammates intend to drop us. Such trust building does not transfer very well to the workplace, where trust in intentions is primary. What our teammates intend in the relatively low stakes of the game may be very different from what they intend with a lot on the line at work.

The best way to build trust is to go right at it, but in the past we have not known enough about trust to do this without causing others to tighten up and to respond defensively—in other words, to create distrust. This is still a problem, but processes like the following can help. Any method we use, however, requires that we enter it with candor, courage, and compassion. We must take the risk of revealing ourselves to get the cooperation that we need. And we must also truly concern ourselves with the other person's best interests as well. As I said in an earlier chapter, we must not only be committed to a mutual purpose, we must be committed to each other as well.

A Process for Building Trust

Here are some basic steps you can take to help build trust in your organization:

1. Have open discussions about what is needed for the organization, for teamwork, and for the individuals involved. Explore the assumptions that underlie these views. Try to see how others are seeing it and reach agreement.

2. Let others know your intentions as clearly as you can, and provide an accurate assessment of your abilities. Express any constraints on your intention to do what is being expected of you—any competing priorities, for example—and any reservations about your competence in doing what is needed.

When you cannot be helpful in one way, see if you can find another way to make a needed contribution.

3. After another person has self-critiqued as just described and you have done the same, you may express any concerns you have about their intentions or abilities. Be specific. Use examples if possible. It is better to put your concerns in the form of questions, rather than accusations. For example, "Do you think you will really have the time, given that other job?" Or, "Have you had any experience in that?" It creates distrust if you generally assert that you think another person does not care about doing a good job or that you think they are incompetent. Give them the space to respond to your question honestly. An exploration of "What will we do if ___ (specifying possible problem situations)?" can help both of you find ways to talk about intentions and competence in an open manner.

4. Take the time to establish mutually satisfactory agreements. The steps above lead to more realistic expectations and commitments. The climate of openness without judgment allows the team to establish agreements the members can count on.

5. Renegotiate expectations when necessary, but not so frequently that others start to believe they cannot depend on you. Follow through.

6. At regular intervals and at the completion of projects, check out everyone's satisfactions and dissatisfactions. Take the necessary actions to resolve problems and adjust expectations. Strive for a climate where people hold themselves accountable. This is one of the attributes of individualism.

In one top management team I was working with, broken trust within the team was paralyzing the organization. Several of the members were saying that others would have to prove their trustworthiness again. "Trust is like Humpty-Dumpty," one of them said. "Once it is broken, it is hard to put together again." I showed them this process for building trust. They did not really believe it would work, but were willing to give it a try because the stakes were so high. It took two days, and there were many tense moments, but we got there. There was sufficient (not total) trust between the managers to work together in good faith to try to get the organization moving again. At the end of a successful turnaround year, it was difficult for anyone in the group to remember exactly what the problems were. Most meetings were marked by laughter and good will.

These steps have proven to go a long way toward building and maintaining what I call tangible trust agreements. The top management team at Classic Communications has become very effective in using this process. Several partners at Booz · Allen & Hamilton used it in building better trust. I have also used it effectively with groups of assembly line workers at Abbott Labs. As a leader in your organizations, you can suggest the process and practice the behaviors yourself. In a short time, this can become a comfortable norm throughout an organization. Let's look again at our communication double helix illustration, but this time adding the dimension of trust.

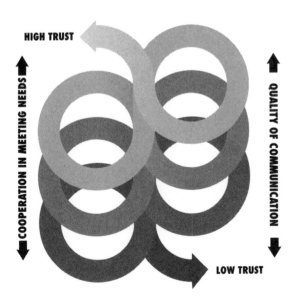

HOW TO USE THESE PROCESSES

The information and practices presented in this chapter are sufficient to build a culture of communication and trust, provided that there are not severe trust problems with higher management. That kind of distrust usually comes from strategies and policies that serve some interests at the expense of others. As we have discovered, if distrust in leadership is determined to be a problem in your organization, you must first do what it takes to establish convergent goals. It is also usually necessary to enlist the services of a top-notch outside organization development consultant. But when relatively widespread trust in higher management exists, the practices described here will take care of most of the communication and trust issues involved in achieving teamwork throughout the organization.

Unleashing the Energy of Commitment

10

Halfhearted commitment is costly. Very costly! Yet frequently, this cost is invisible. How often do we leave a meeting feeling a little flat? Nothing was wrong exactly. We did what we came to do. But there is the sense that nothing really happened, and worse, the sense that nothing *will* happen. That's usually a good indicator that we have just been drained by the negative energy of low commitment. When total commitment exists, we tend to leave meetings with excitement and a desire to "get it on." It's like breaking the huddle believing that if we execute on this play we can score!

Top-notch organization development consultants frequently design and lead processes that increase commitment. The results often reach 30 to 50 percent in measurable performance gains, and sometimes much more than that. This indicates the existence of some type of reserve energy waiting to be unleashed. Prior to the intervention, the people involved usually report that they are tired and overworked. They reflect a heavy mixture of doubts and desires, hopes and fears, urgency and caution. But as they begin to talk together about their concerns and discover some practical solutions, the energy in the group begins to lift. A new kind of energy has entered—an emotional energy. And it has significantly increased the amount of physical and intellectual energy available. The catalytic energy of commitment has been unleashed.

To be sure, there is a risk when people are invited to voice their doubts, concerns, and fears, but that is the only way to develop commitment. No matter how rational or profitable the plan, people do not give it the energy of their complete commitment until all of their doubts and concerns are at least explored. When they are left unexplored, and often only partially conscious, such concerns are automatically the catalyst for caution and constraint. Leaders must learn to surface concerns and work through them rather than attempting to dispel them with criticism or overcome them with inspirational rhetoric.

Chapters 7 and 8 provided a comprehensive checklist of commitment issues and a process for working through them. This chapter provides an in-depth understanding of commitment and some of the causes for a lack of it. It applies this understanding to 10 of the specific types of constrained commitment and provides strategies and tools that leaders can use in surfacing them and resolving them. This is not just about solving problems, but the process of surfacing and resolving concerns and doubt is the action that unleashes the extra energy of commitment.

UNDERSTANDING COMMITMENT

The opposite of commitment is not freedom, as many have supposed. It is caution and constraint blocking the free flow of spirit and energy. To commit means to put something in or to pledge it. The opposite is to omit—to withhold something or leave it out. When we do not commit, we are bound in the chains of our own hesitation. Omit me, they say. Commitment is the catalyst that frees us to take action, to dance out our dreams.

Commitment and love are close kin. The popular song "The Rose," written by Amanda McBroom and popularized by Bette Midler, captures this. It describes the costs of holding back, of not giving ourselves. And like the love described in the song, commitment leads to the blooming of our highest and most beautiful potentials. It frees us to live! One philosopher said that the secret to a fulfilling life is to be totally committed, knowing that your commitment is totally tentative. Human beings want to commit. It feels good. They also want the commitment of others. Commitment is natural.

So why do people hold back? What's behind the ever-ready "wait-and-see" attitude? There are two key causes for holding back, for withholding commitment. One is caution; the other is over-commitment, or competing commitments. Over-commitment is best dealt with through open, accountable discussions about what people are willing and able to do. Caution is the more common and costly reason for withholding commitment.

Like commitment, caution is also natural, built into the human apparatus. We are engineered that way. Caution and commitment are both natural states tied to built-in chemical-emotional process-es. One of those processes could be called the chemistry of trust; the other the chemistry of fear. The extreme example of the chemically driven process of fear happens when the body releases a great deal of adrenaline into the bloodstream, preparing us for strong action like fight, flight, or freeze. This chemical-emotional reaction is designed to protect us by giving us an extra surge of energy to aggres-sively attack or rapidly retreat. The reaction of caution is a milder chemical-emotional process, but it is also designed to protect us by, in this case, holding us back. You can feel the chemistry of caution in the sensation of tightening up, of energizing protective force fields. Putting up walls, it is called. It does not feel particularly good, but paradoxically, we feel safer, whether we truly are or not.

Trust is another natural chemical-emotional process, and it is the condition that precedes commitment. In the movie *Bull Durham*, the seasoned catcher tells the young pitcher that what a player needs in the majors is an equal amount of fear and arrogance. To some degree, this statement captures these two opposite natural states. Arrogance is an extreme form of confidence or trust in being able to do whatever it takes. The actual events of the movie, however, cap-tured more. The young cocky pitcher had gotten good enough to go to the majors by learning to trust the catcher and his other team-mates. A degree of fear and a whole lot of trust would perhaps be a better prescription for playing in the big leagues of anything.

But commitment may be even more mysterious and interesting than that. What if we think of love, in all its forms, as the force of attraction that pulls things together—a kind of spiritual-emotional gravity called desire? And fear or caution as the force that pushes things apart? Trust, then, is the mediating force that breaks through caution, enabling the choice of commitment. Commitment is the force that binds things together. Commitment is love in action.

In close personal relations, we already know the truth of this, but it is also true at work. The power of loving your work has been known forever. But it goes further. Organizations can be defined as people coming together to achieve certain purposes. If there is disagreement about those purposes, if people feel like the organization's purposes are being served, but their purposes are being ignored, they hold back. Caution and sometimes fear will rule. But when they are attracted to the same purposes, when purposes become mutual or at least reciprocal, and when trust in the leaders exists, people become committed. And the power of love propels the organization.

The prerequisite for commitment is choice. Based on the degree of trust and confidence people feel—or conversely, the degree of caution, concern, or fear they are experiencing—people choose to commit themselves or to hold back. Commitment cannot be com-manded. It must be earned the old-fashioned way—one employee at a time. Only compliance can be commanded, and as we know, that has very little power.

Interestingly, this is one reason why strong individualism is so critical to organizations today. Strong individuals either commit or openly voice their concerns. It all begins with the individual. Weak individuals or go-along team players, on the other hand, make weak commitments without voicing their concerns.

Commitment does not begin with "total" however. It is given by degrees. A common managerial (and marital) mistake is to think of commitment as a total condition, a "yes or no" condition. We are either committed or we are not. But in these relationships and in all of daily human life, commitment is an ongoing process of choice that results in the degree of energy and intention we put into a thing. The "yes/no" choice often occurs only at the beginning and at the end. We choose to join the organization, take the job, or get married. We choose to resign, look for work elsewhere, or get a divorce. In between, we decide the degree of our commitment to the people and activities involved.

Most of us do not flatly say "no" to our boss or to the team. We give a halfhearted "yes," and that is precisely what is so costly. Efforts continue to get less than what is required or what they deserved. But this is not admitted. What is needed for vital organizational work and personal living is wholehearted commitment. That is what yields the huge performance gains.

Total commitment is the essence of the pioneer spirit. For pioneers, commitment is not optional. They must decide a course of action and then give it their full attention and intention. They must be dedicated to the actions they take. Hesitation and doubt can be deadly. No less will be required of 21st century organizations.

"So how do we get that to happen?" many of you will be saying. "We've tried the consensus thing. Is there more?" Yes, there is. The "more" that is required is leadership that deeply understands the truth of individual human choice and therefore commits to the task of continuously surfacing and resolving doubts and concerns. The foundation for commitment is strong when it is solidly built on the rock of doubts, fears, and concerns that have been through the "furnace" of open discussion and welded into the steel of resolve. When they are ignored or suppressed, these concerns become the swampy muck that can bog down any project or the shifting sands that can topple any organization.

Three words of caution, however, before you start working to build commitment. First, it is clear that hesitation or weak action in today's rapidly changing marketplace can be deadly. Leaders must therefore be skilled in ways of surfacing and resolving concerns, with resolutions that move quickly into strong action and that keep the action moving. For example, the popular belief that "keeping options open" is a good reason to not fully commit can be countered by asking for a commitment to an intensive exploration of the options.

The second caution is that strong individual commitment to the organization or to teamwork can lead to resentment. Increased commitment necessarily increases the degree of interdependence and consequently the expectations on others. Most organizational conflicts (and most marital problems) are simply variations of this phenomenon. When calling forth commitment, therefore, it is imperative that you follow through. Otherwise, you would be better off to let well enough alone and accept the mediocrity of halfhearted compliance. It is usually less visible.

Finally, in addition to a commitment to follow through, leaders must demonstrate their commitment to the organization and particularly to the individuals and teams who do the work. It is not enough to merely be committed to goals and objectives. That does not inspire trust, it inspires caution. Furthermore, any self-serving lack of commitment to the organization will be sensed by others and will serve as a model for low commitment throughout.

There are always legitimate doubts and concerns that need to be worked through in every organization and about most projects. They are cause for legitimate caution and a legitimate form of low commitment. They should be respected, discussed, and worked through. What follows now is a description of 10 common types of low commitment that often arise more from habitual negative beliefs and attitudes than from legitimate organizational or individual concerns. As such, they are more like "games" and consequently require leadership interventions to prevent them from choking committed energy out of an organization.

TEN TYPES OF HABITUAL LOW COMMITMENT

The following types of less than legitimate low commitment are found in most organizations of any size. I'll analyze each type, indicating the kinds of actions leaders can take to counter them. More is required, however, than the piecemeal application of these concepts. That's why we have outlined with a checklist the comprehensive strategies for developing a culture of commitment in organizations. So let's consider these further impediments to commitment to expand on the actions already considered.

1. Reactions to Perceived Conditions

Three perceived conditions facing organizations affect management choices and the degree of commitment from employees. Those three *perceived* conditions are

- the degree of safety,
- the degree of predictability, and
- the degree of resource sufficiency.

Concerns about these conditions are legitimate, but frequently they come from ingrained thought patterns and have little to do with reality. In either case, the needed leadership intervention is essentially the same.

Most people try to maintain a certain margin of safety most of the time. Most people desire some degree of both continuity and change. Most people are afraid of scarcity and will try to conserve, particularly with resources that they perceive to belong to them. When a situation seems hopeless, when the danger feels too great, when there is too much change too quickly or too much boring continuity, or when resources seem inadequate to the task, people tend to hold back.

The solution to this kind of constrained commitment starts with leaders asking employees about their perceptions, and making those perceptions discussible in team meetings. When the leader conveys an intention of looking for the best course of action (rather than merely listening to complaints), such discussions lead to a more optimistic group perception as members see new possibilities and new ways to work together to overcome their common problems. This leads to higher levels of commitment. Even when the picture still looks bleak, convergent leaders learn to use such discussions to catalyze a form of "up against the wall" commitment.

There is another way in which perceived conditions constrain commitment. Employees tend to hold back when their perceptions of conditions differ too radically from management's perceptions— ones that have either been stated by the managers or seem to be implied by the programs the managers are pursuing. Alignment of perceptions is the answer here. Again, open discussions are the key. Managers should share their own perceptions, supporting them with data when possible, but they must not try to sell their way of seeing things. It is just as important for them to listen to employee perceptions and to inquire about employee data. An honest, open give-and-take can lead to shared perceptions and shared vision. That sets the stage for high levels of commitment.

2. The Energy Savers

Every organization has its share of people who are saving their energy for after-hours activities. In factories, this is called "give 'em eight and hit the gate." In knowledge work, the Internet and computer games get increasing action as the close of the business day nears. Others, including managers, can be heard discussing golf, families, or weekend plans. Not all of these behaviors indicate low commitment, but when people routinely engage in them, their commitment to the job is obviously low. And their behavior is catching.

Douglas McGregor saw such people in terms of their motivations.[13] It was not that they lacked motivation, he contended, but that they were motivated by things other than work. That does not account for all of the phenomenon. Many people who lead very active lives after work display a high degree of energy and commitment on the job. You can feel their enthusiasm. And when they leave for Little League, a run by the lake, or an early dinner with their valentine, you can feel their enthusiasm for that too.

On the other hand, when asked about their energy when leaving work, most energy savers acknowledge that they leave feeling tired, with little inclination to do anything. Their energy-saving strategies are not working. When energy saving is perceived, leaders can often turn it around by suggesting that everyone engage in an experiment to see if they feel more energy on days that they give their full attention and energy to their jobs or on days that they daydream and take it easy. Most will find that energy generates energy and loafing drains it. They had inherited the belief that the opposite was true but never tested it in their own lives. Some high performers have been created by this experiment. Even workers who perform hard continuous labor learn to pace their energy, not save it.

3. Hot Rock Managers

One manufacturing manager I know comes into nearly every meeting with an announcement that he will have to leave early—to attend another meeting. Many of these meetings are for the purpose of increasing production rates or lowering reject rates on the manufacturing line for which he has responsibility.

After his customary announcement, he tends to sit down and engage in joking around with those in attendance, but fidgets as if he were sitting on a hot rock. The meetings proceed typically with the leader of that particular team (often cross-functional) moving down the list of pre-published agenda items, asking various people to report. A few questions are asked. A few people volunteer to look into certain things and report back at the next meeting. Occasionally, someone suggests a new procedure; seldom does this result in discussion, action planning, or the assignment of responsibility. That only happens when they have a consultant facilitate an off-site retreat for them. Then they are somehow freed from their restlessness.

At some point, usually right after an agenda item is "completed," the manufacturing manager leaves the room early. He is careful to be unobtrusive about his departure. No one seems to mind. In fact, several of them may have come late or left early themselves—to attend another meeting of course. The most surprising thing is that our manufacturing manager does this even in his boss's meetings. And his boss does it too. No one is committed to the meetings, much less to any plans that might accidentally emerge from them. Apparently, all of them are committed to the appointment books embedded in their various computers. Somebody in some time-management course must have sold them on this powerful management tool. Like worms on hot rocks, they can hardly bear being in meetings. They squirm to get away to the next meeting.

The cure is, of course, for someone to actually become committed to and a bit demanding about these meetings. Or stop having them. That would greatly relieve managers' schedules so they might actually be able to focus on what they need to do to get better results.

4. Making Certain vs. Making Happen

A lot of teams, particularly in technical organizations, play a computer game that could be called "Data Dodge Ball." When looking into any problem or considering any action, they measure everything—and then measure everything else—and then do it again. Various numbers are flashed on the screen, and first one functional group or another grabs one of these "data balls" and throws it at one of the other groups. The "target group" of course dodges. Seldom does anyone take a direct hit, so the game tends to last a long time.

When not throwing data balls, group members work the numbers in every conceivable way. Frequently, they are still not convinced they have found the true core cause, and in frustration they become uncertain that they have even pinpointed the right problem. So they study it some more. They are clearly not ready to commit to a course of action. The game then ends in something akin to Pareto prioritizing paralysis—a very low energy state indeed.

An individual form of this low commitment phenomenon could be called "being right vs. being committed." This game works pretty much the same as the one above, except that the combatants are typically "experts" in the same field rather than cross-functional adversaries. For a time, this version seems to yield a lot of energy, even passion. A form of commitment is operating, but it is aimed at being right, not at being committed to a common course of action to solve a problem. I worked with one group in which the design engineers involved had been at this game for nearly seven years. The available energy had turned to cross-canceling anger. The breakthrough was to challenge them to try all of the solutions being advocated. When they did, they got results, and even though they did not know which solution had helped the most, the true energy of commitment was unleashed toward even better solutions.

The correction to both situations described here is for someone in a leadership role to challenge those involved to *try something!* "It is bias for action," as Tom Peters described it in *In Search of Excellence*.[14] If the study phase has gone through more than two typical cycles of whatever is being studied, the group is likely drifting toward infinite loop. It is time to just "boot it."

Often, the best way to get everyone committed to some kind of action is to establish a sense of fair play by trying every suggestion that has any strong advocates. This is what I call "the 100 percent solution." It broke the deadlock in the case described above. The common objection to this is cost. That is purportedly why Pareto was in play. However, seven years of deadlock were considerably more expensive than doing everything people could think of to solve the problem. And, as is often the case, in only a few months the members proved that trying everything cost less than the production lost.

5. *"Understanding" Managers*

These managers are also referred to as "accepting," "laid-back," and "easy going." Generally, employees praise their compassion, understanding, and likable personalities. In confidential interviews, however, many employees also express frustration at the inability or unwillingness of such managers to confront the excuses of some employees for their lack of teamwork or poor performance. As a result, even though the loyalty to these managers tends to be high, the energy of those they supervise tends to be low. When they are leading cross-functional teams, dread becomes the primary emotion of those involved, and avoidance becomes their primary behavior.

The managers of such managers are usually quite aware of the supervisee's leadership problems and frequently frustrated in their efforts to provide coaching in more performance-based behaviors. They also find these managers likable and are therefore reluctant to simply demote them or to keep them at the same salary level while relieving them of managerial responsibility. Consequently, they keep trying things, but have difficulty knowing exactly what needs to change for these protégés to be more effective leaders.

One reason it is so difficult to deal with "understanding" managers is that there are at least three variations of the type, with only subtle differences in apparent behavior, but profound differences in motivation. The common thread that makes the three types look so similar is the easy-going acceptance of the behaviors of those they supervise, even when those behaviors are detrimental to teamwork or to the success of a project. The resulting low commitment and energy of their teams is another common thread. There are great differences in motivation behind the three types, however, requiring very different solutions.

The first type is the one that is most commonly the diagnosis of employees and the managers' managers. This type can be called *the conflict avoiders*. Somewhere back in their childhood, such managers got the message that conflict was a bad thing and that all differences and disagreements inevitably led to conflict. Such managers are committed to keeping things safe. This is the most difficult type to correct. It requires a change of belief. The manager must come to believe that differences and disagreements can be openly discussed without always leading to conflict, and that when conflict does occur, it can be productively managed. Sometimes this new belief can be formed by simply helping the conflict avoider observe and process their own personal experience in participating in successful, even enjoyable meetings in which strong differences of opinion are surfaced and worked through. Often, however, such managers must have the repeated experience of *leading* such meetings, initially with a mentor or coach there as a safety net.

The second type is much easier to correct. We will call them *the process challenged*. Such managers frequently have strong opinions and are comfortably assertive in stating them and in challenging the opinions of those they supervise, but mostly in one-on-one settings. In group settings, they are unaware of subtle signs that disagreements exist, and they lack the skills to get them out in the open and dealt with even when they do see them. Such managers are frequently committed to the *content* but clueless about *process*. Many managers from technical backgrounds fall into this category. The solution here is training. Role-play practice will be required.

The third type I call *the sandbaggers*. Such managers are committed to keeping performance expectations (those expected of them) in the safely achievable range. They fear that if they achieve "stretch goals" their bosses will then raise the bar beyond their stretch. Their fear of success is that it will lead to failure. They are therefore very "understanding" of all employee reasons why more demanding goals should not be set. They quickly accept "acts of God," unexplained natural cycles, and a very broad definition of what is outside their group's control. They use these reasons to assertively argue for goals that do not push "their people" to the breaking point. The solution here is for such a manager's manager to not mirror these accepting behaviors, but instead to engage their supervisee in setting realistically achievable stretch goals and in continuing to look for ways to improve even beyond those.

Even though the motivations and solutions are different, the impact of "understanding" managers is usually the same: low challenge, low commitment, low energy. In each case, the correction must result in their leading group processes in which doubts and differences are surfaced, worked through, and resolved. Only then will they be able to unleash the energy of commitment in the groups they manage.

6. Crisis Managers

Curiously, crisis managers are commonly misunderstood. It is believed that they are committed but ineffective, that the very intensity of their commitment causes them to constantly overreact. And in a sense this is true. Crisis managers (like two of the types of "understanding" managers above) are committed to protecting themselves, to keeping themselves safe from situations and expectations they fear they cannot handle. They use crises, therefore, and the heroic actions they lead as a smoke screen to hide their lack of commitment to real organizational results. The solution is to not be deceived by the smoke screen and to insist on accomplishment, not agitated action.

7. Employeeism: The Boss-Flunky Syndrome

A great many people, particularly in class-conscious cultures, have been conditioned to see the world in terms of bosses who give orders and flunkies who follow them. This produces a syndrome of passive-aggressive behavior that could also be called employeeism. "Don't expect initiative or commitment from me, I just work here," we can almost hear these employees say through their postures and expressions. Energy is not only low, it is sullen. This cultural phenomenon has been declining over the last 20 years of participative management practices, but pockets of it still remain. This attitude takes some time to overcome, but once it has been eliminated, the change is usually permanent. Leaders who consistently engage employees in collaborative planning, listening to and respecting their ideas and trusting in the process enough to refrain from rescuing the group by making the decisions themselves, will find that in time a new culture of mutual responsibility will emerge. With this will come increased commitment with all its extra energy.

8. Territorial Teams

In Chapter 5, some of the undesirable side effects of the team fad were described. One of them involved team collusion in developing territorial strategies against the expectations of other groups—some of them customers of the team's products and services. Another involved peer pressure on high performers to do less. Both of these are advocated under the banner of commitment, but it is commitment to misconceived team protectionist tactics rather than commitment to results that are in the best interest of all. These have the same organizational impacts as low commitment and low energy. Maybe even worse, since they are a kind of counter-commitment. To combat this, I proposed a focus on teamwork rather than teams. It also helps for leaders to institute improvement efforts that are results-oriented, systems-focused, and measured by aligned goals.

9. The HRM Hedge

In the last 25 years, Human Resources (previously Personnel) has become increasingly powerful, due mostly to the fact that they protect their organizations from the legal dangers of practices that could be construed as "unfair." Beyond the legal issues, being fair is important, but in far too many instances, some employees are unfairly hiding behind this HRM protection. They are hedging their commitment to projects, other team members, improvement efforts, and learning anything more than what they know right this minute (unless the meter for additional compensation starts the minute they learn it). They also hide behind this HRM hedge when they refuse to commit to work with someone better qualified than they who got the promotion they wanted. And on and on.

When I conduct individual interviews in preparation for an improvement project, I usually hear about a few employees who are using these tactics to gum up the works for everyone else. Unfortunately, HR usually does not seem to catch on to this and responds to the trouble that these few cause with ever more audits and more rules to audit. In too many organizations, fairness is coming to mean "penalize everyone equally," except for these chronically uncommitted few. The solution is for HRM to get squarely into the commitment and accountability business—as well as the fairness business—and for organizational leaders to insist that they do so.

10. FYI—Only

Far too many meetings are happening these days—meetings in which nothing happens but the meeting. I opened the chapter by describing the debilitating effect of such meetings. Many of them are cross-functional, weekly updates and information exchanges regarding progress, or the lack thereof, in achieving mutually established improvement goals. This should be cause for increasing commitment, not diminishing it. Often, the project was launched with a committed intention on the part of all parties participating. What went wrong? For some reason, participants have lost their willingness to openly surface their doubts, concerns, and disagreements. When progress falters, therefore, they use the weekly meetings to look at charts and speculate about reasons. But they no longer engage openly, hash out differences, and commit to new actions.

What could have prevented this? Fewer meetings is part of the answer. It is too easy for weekly meetings to become routine—for participants to come in straight from their daily detail overload, distracted by thinking about what they must do after the meeting. As a result, they get in the habit of staying in their comfort zones, deciding there will be time next meeting to really push to find out what is going wrong with this improvement project. And next time it goes the same way. It becomes habit, to the point that no matter how open they had been in the beginning, they do not know how to get there again.

A good solution is to stop having the routine, weekly, one-hour meetings and instead plan meetings that are long enough to dig in, work things through, and come out again in a committed action mode. This usually takes a minimum of three hours, even with limited scope. The increase in commitment and results more than pay for the time.

THE COMMITMENT DIFFERENCE

Commitment is a catalyst that can unleash incredible levels of extra energy. Initially, this extra energy is emotional energy, but that is only the primer for tremendous surges of intellectual and physical energy as well. With this boost, individuals and teams are able to achieve things that were seemingly impossible. They are able to achieve the pioneering visions that can make life better for all of us.

Changing
Leadership Beliefs

11

T he effort to achieve the convergence of interests required for pioneering must begin with an organization's leaders. Interestingly, the first step many leaders must take is to change themselves. And that means changing the way they think, first and foremost, so they can overcome traditional thinking patterns that hinder rather than help convergence.

MIRED IN OLD BELIEFS

A strange streak of irrationality afflicts many leaders today. In spite of repeated evidence that involvement and convergence works, they revert back to their old organizational thinking and their old management ways. Perhaps many of them know better, but do not feel they can buck the limited interests of investment analysts and the finance domination in far too many business schools. Or perhaps they lack the pioneering individualism to break free.

A more common reason, I believe, is an inability to break the stranglehold of certain kinds of old beliefs. These beliefs function more like an operating system than an application. Somehow these leaders are not able to believe the power of convergence, even though they have personally witnessed extraordinary results. The new data will just not run on their old code. This chapter is designed to help leaders change these old beliefs—to upgrade their mental software.

Two beliefs are causing most of the problems: beliefs about change and beliefs about organizations and how they should be managed. These beliefs hinder convergence and pioneering and should be altered.

A NEW VIEW OF CHANGE

Change is not what it used to be. We once thought of change as the exception and constants as the rule. Now everyone is saying that change is the only constant. We were wrong both times.

Change is the modification of something or the transformation of it into something new. The operative word here is *thing*. Things exist. Everything that exists, that is existence, is made up of three interacting forces. Change is one of them. It *is* a constant force in existence. Its dynamic opposite is continuity, the cohesive force of holding things together. Continuity is also a constant force in existence. The third force, causality, creates conditions that establish the direction and degree of change needed and specifications for what should be retained. That is, causality triggers change in *things*, but also encourages continuities.

There are two types of causality—chance and choice. [Chance is being used here perhaps a bit unfairly to characterize not just randomness, but also the laws of science, both physical and biological, and also the new "laws" of chaos. Even though some of the changes of this type can be calculated and predicted with mathematical methods, they all still have in common that they are resulting from causes outside of human choice.] Chance rules all things that are not conscious. Choice plays a decisive role when consciousness is involved. These three forces are in play at all times, and everything that exists, exists because of them. Their intertwining relationship is the story of the universe.

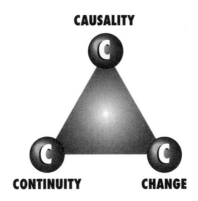

CAUSALITY

CONTINUITY   **CHANGE**

The laws of thermodynamics were only partially right. The theory of force-field analysis that was based on them is similarly flawed. Things are not seeking a state of equilibrium. There is no state of equilibrium, or stasis. There is no "stop" point. All things in existence are constantly evolving in form, some characteristics continuing and some changing. Anything staying the same is discarded or dies. Anything changed too much dissipates or is destroyed. With chance, it's a 50/50 proposition, or survival of the fittest only. With consciousness, we have a choice. The universe is not seeking equilibrium; it is seeking an expansion of cohesive material creation. It is my conviction that the nature of the universe is conscious creation and that its expansion is infinite. Shall we choose to join it?

It Is Not Change I'm Resisting!

People do not resist change, they resist loss. People do not resist change per se; they welcome *beneficial* change. Human beings have a built-in need for both continuity and change. If things stay too much the same, they get tired and bored. They love novelty. They also love familiarity and continuities they can count on. Yes, some are more one way than the other. Individualists are, for example, the best suited for change. Even so, all human beings have some mixture of both. We have built into us systems that support both self-preservation and growth.

Even more fundamental is the fact that all things exist as a natural bonding of continuity and change, not a triumph of one over the other. They exist as a result of three forces, not two. The dynamic throughout existence is toward change and growth that preserves elements from the past. The universe does not just start over. At least it has not since the Big Bang, if something like that did indeed occur. The universe seeks both conservation and creation. It is not a zero-sum game. Leaders who are truly interested in taking responsibility for their organizations, not just the bottom line, would do well to notice this dynamic and be guided by it.

Change and the Legacy of a Power Struggle

We have examined the power struggle within organizations between the goals of leaders, individuals, and teams. This power struggle is fed by a focus on only two of the three forces, the *gain* of something by one of these entities (a changed state) and the *resistance* of the others. There is little attempt to examine one's own motives as the cause of such change. Intuitively, we have always known that people put up resistance when they expect to lose something they do not want to lose. Today, strangely, a great many leaders pursuing change initiatives seem to assume that the changes will be beneficial or at least benign, and they delude themselves into imagining some perverse and mysterious psychological condition called "resistance to change" and the need for a shaman to cure it. The power struggle that is then created is totally antithetical to positive change.

Here are the forms the power struggle has taken in relation to change:

1. *Dictatorships*: The leader pursues change that creates a loss for both individuals and groups and that also attempts to overthrow what has existed. Anticipating resistance, the leader creates methods to crush it.

2. *Aristocratic*: The leader allies with strong individualists to pursue change that creates loss for social groups. Then those in power use methods designed to suppress or overwhelm the formation of resistance groups.

3. *Collectivists*: The leader allies with strong groups to pursue change that creates loss for individuals. Mind control and suppression of individual initiatives are common tools.

4. *Me-ism*: Individuals pursue change that creates loss for groups and may also create loss for the organization. Success at this usually involves covert methods.

5. *Territorial Teams*: Groups create strong internal loyalties to protect their group's status quo or sometimes to pursue changes that benefit their group at the expense of individuals and the organization. Peer pressure and confrontational methods are used, and if they fail, either disruption or passive resistance then follows.

Change Propaganda

We need to forget most of what we have heard about change. The topic has become encased in propaganda. Some of it is innocent, resulting from inadequate partial theories, but a great deal of it is used to conceal or justify selfish motives. This second type is the product of an age in which it is no longer fashionable to conquer and enslave or to coerce with fear tactics, but even in its euphemistic forms it still boils down to the few trying to benefit themselves at the expense of others. Here are four examples of change propaganda.

Omniscience

Omniscience is a view of change promoted by a great many writers and consultants. They write about resistance to change as if it were some form of psychological weakness in people—a sort of neurosis that would be cured if those people would only listen to these writers and realize that change is good, and that aligning with the purpose of change will make everything turn out well. These writers, of course, from their omniscient perches, *know* that change is good and that all will turn out well. And that is simply absurd. Change that is significant and real risks the unknown, and anyone with good sense would exercise a fair amount of caution.

I realized this one day when I had just come from a meeting with a top management group that had spent months planning some change strategies for their organization. Everything about the meeting was difficult. People were testy. They were making threats about "anybody" who did not do their part, and they were finding reasons to delay the launch. Reflecting on the meeting, it suddenly dawned on me, that they were resisting the change that they themselves were causing. In the next meeting, I helped them surface their fears and face them. It was clear that nobody was sure how it would turn out, but it still seemed worth the risks. They made some improvements to their plan and launched it. It succeeded, I think, largely because of the protective improvements they included in the strategy and because of the fact that the experience resulted in their taking the concerns of their employees more seriously.

Absent-mindedness

Absent-mindedness is a view of change that results from "change agents" who do not notice that the change is defined from their reference point. They blithely pull out their force-field analysis and begin to list change enablers and resistance forces and how they will deal with the resistance. They somehow seem unaware that they are causing the change and fail to examine their own motives, except in terms of convincing a few of the resistors that their motives are pure, thereby attempting to neutralize resistance.

Spin Doctoring

Spin masters promote a view of change that conceals the fact that their leaders are causing change that creates loss for others. They describe the change in terms of market forces or forces of nature. This is the self-regulating/*laissez faire* view.

Change Management

Many change managers advance arguments about the benefits of the change, making sure to call a press conference and subject employees to indoctrination training sessions. The changes are often being caused by the purchase of state-of-the-art technologies that unfortunately leave little room for local customization. This is a form of authoritarian leadership, and the change managers are often playing the role of "occupation" forces.

Conscious Convergent Change

The word *convergent* implies its opposite, *divergent*. The dictionary defines *divergent* as a turning of the eyes outward away from each other. I intend for *convergent* to mean *exactly* the opposite of that—a turning of the eyes inward toward each other. It means to stop blaming change on natural laws or on market forces and to start taking responsibility for change and the losses it can create. It suggests a search for a convergence of interests. Such a search takes the form of deliberations with all involved to maximize the gains and minimize the losses for everyone. When this is done, after-the-fact change "management" can be a thing of the past.

The word *conscious* is added to help us remember the chance or choice option, and that choice comes as a result of consciousness. Therefore, creating greater consciousness is a very practical goal. Greater consciousness creates better solutions and more committed contribution. It is the source of vision, particularly pioneering vision.

At Vignette, CEO Greg Peters makes a distinction that helps in seeking a convergence of interests in the face of change. "People confuse culture with how a culture manifests to an individual at a particular time. When we reached the point that it was more effective to stabalize roles and specialize, some employees felt like we were losing an important part of our culture—the willingness to just do what it takes to get things done. When we were small, a person might work in support one day, MIS the next, and product development the next. But that role-shifting was not our culture, it was a manifestation of our culture, and it was not scalable. The attitude of doing what is needed, is our culture, and it is very scalable." This distinction helped Vignette work through some changing conditions in a way that the perception of loss diminished.

The purpose of this discussion is to correct some faulty thinking about change and to create a fuller understanding of it. It is hoped that this will help you see the opportunity and the need for planning convergent change. It may also help you see that changing at the speed of choice rather than managing at the speed of change is a better idea. My experience of doing so is that it is slow going at first, but that it then enables implementation to proceed at warp speed.

A NEW VIEW OF ORGANIZATIONS

The prevailing beliefs about organizations are derived from scientific theories of the universe and its functioning, not from our direct experience in organizations. These were once considered "modern" beliefs, but are now the old ones I was referring to in the first part of this chapter. They were once the new beliefs that replaced the old medieval beliefs. They allowed us to accomplish many things through organizations that we would not have been able to accomplish without them. They now stand in the way of our journey into the new millennium and the accomplishments that are needed now. Unfortunately, the old beliefs are foundational and very difficult to change. They are tied to our most basic beliefs about the universe—paradigms they are called.

Yes, I know a few jokes about the word *paradigm* too. Unfortunately, I heard them from people who were not aware that in telling the jokes, their paradigms were showing. Paradigms are deadly serious. They account for a high percentage of the errors made by leaders. They also account for many instances of success. Nations, companies, and individuals thrive or die by their paradigms.

The word *paradigm* describes a phenomenon that is very similar to our most basic and usually unconscious assumptions. These assumptions are a form of mental organization that not only enables us to make sense out of the thousands of unstructured stimuli bombarding our senses every second of our lives, but in a very real sense they give the unstructured stimuli their structure. Without paradigms, we would not be able to function. Paradigms are our most basic understanding of the nature of reality. They determine the patterns we are able to see, but also block us from seeing other patterns with an equal claim to reality. They even determine many of the objects and events we see or miss seeing.

To illustrate, there is an account of some 15th century native people who had no concept of and therefore could not see the European ship with the great white sails anchored in their bay. There is no account of what they did see in that space, but we may imagine it had something to do with water. We can speculate that their paradigm was water centered—fish swimming in it and small boats struggling around precariously on top of it. We can further speculate that this water paradigm perhaps did not sufficiently account for the water's relationship to the wind that filled those great white sails and moved the ship over vast expanses of ocean. Since they could not account for the sails, they could not see them! Worse, what they could not conceive of and therefore could not see conquered them. Perhaps we should use a catchy phrase to capture the role these conceptual templates called paradigms play. *Vision blindness* is a phrase that comes fairly close to describing the paradoxical function of paradigms.

Paradigms are behind what is wrong with the world, but also what is right with it. They serve as universal guides that show us what to create, but also suggest what it is permissible to exploit or destroy. Furthermore, they determine the things we do under the banner of leadership. It is my thesis that leaders often do not see what is needed due to their paradigms. This could become increasingly so in the future. The reason is that the dominant paradigms of our time will not serve managers in leading 21st century organizations. These paradigms are limited by some very dangerous blind spots.

The Dominant Paradigms

In the 20th century, there have been three dominant paradigms that have shaped thinking and action. They are the *mechanistic, organic, and relativistic* paradigms.[15] These three emerged from and served as foundations for the scientific revolution. They replaced an earlier paradigm that was religious or ecclesiastic in nature, which had, in turn, replaced one that was more tribal. Each of the three took us a long way in seeing new truths and new possibilities. Furthermore, perhaps for the first time, each new paradigm built on the preceding one rather then replacing it. Collectively, they could be called the scientific paradigm. Together, they allowed us to see "objective," or "outer," reality more clearly. But none of these individually, nor all of them collectively, are sufficient to serve our needs now. They have made us blind to some very important organizational forces. We need a new paradigm.

Let's briefly consider these three paradigms and the beliefs about organizations that came from them. These beliefs are shaped by what the paradigms allowed us to see and also what they caused us to miss.

The Mechanistic Paradigm

This paradigm allowed us to see and mathematically predict the physical motion of the universe. From this came the sciences of physics and mathematics, as well as miraculous machines that made it possible for human beings to accomplish amazing new feats. It was natural for us, therefore, to begin to think of organizations as machines too, and the people who worked in them as replaceable parts. Unfortunately, this mechanical view of things blinded us to our own living reality.

The Organic Paradigm

This paradigm was biology's answer to the "hard" sciences. It too was built on scientific principles, but it insisted that any view of the universe must include an explanation of living things. This allowed us to see the transformative changes known as evolution and put us back in touch with the birth, growth, and death of living things. Our view of organizations softened. Organizations were not machines, but instead were environments for living organisms that required care and feeding. We came to see organizations as something like nurseries or farms. The unfortunate part was that we started to think of individual employees as farm animals and teams as herds. We became blind to the fact that they had some choice in the matter and were capable of feeding themselves.

The Relativistic Paradigm

This paradigm began to emerge as an explanation of the unexplained and the unexpected. The other two sciences had mapped the universe and provided a rational explanation for practically everything in it, but there were anomalies. Einstein, Heisenberg, and others began to explore this unknown. We began to see the systems dance going on in the universe; we formulated chaos theory; and organizations began to appear as intricate energy patterns. It was a dazzling view of things. The unfortunate part was that from this cosmic perspective, individuals began to be confused with atoms and teams with molecules. They just needed to trust the process. We were so dazzled that something so small as an employee's doubts and fears became invisible. Once again, scientific objectivity had blinded us to the evidence of our own reality.

What's Wrong with This Picture?

The main thing wrong with these three pictures separately, and with the composite picture presented by the scientific paradigm they collectively constitute, is that they blind us to the two most obvious things in the landscape:

1) Consciousness creates choice, and

2) Being aware, people make choices.

These are the white sails that because of the dominant paradigms of our time, leaders are unable to see, or see only dimly. Perhaps in the vast reaches of cosmic explanation they are not so obvious, but at the systems level of human society and human organization, they are the dominant features.

Peter Block, in his book *Stewardship*, offers an explanation for "why we don't act on what we know" about organizational effectiveness. He describes managers as similar to authoritarian leaders and suggests that in them "what remains untouched (by the evidence) is the belief that power and purpose and privilege can reside at the top and the organization can still learn how to serve its stakeholders and therefore survive."[16] I would add that this belief does not change because of the way organizations, individuals, teams, and leadership are implicitly viewed in the three dominant paradigms. Leaders see the evidence of breakthroughs that come from acting on the understanding that people are aware and make choices. They even praise the programs that bring them about. But most of their actions are still ruled by the deterministic scientific paradigms. They just cannot "unbelieve" their paradigmatic biases about the nature of organizations and how one should lead them. And so they keep on doing the same old things with the same old results. This is the source of most management error.

Let me be more specific. Mechanistic Paradigm (MP) leaders are fixated on the "machine." They worry about getting the design (structure) and mechanics right and about enough documented procedures to maintain control of it. These are rational matters; emotion only gets in the way (this in spite of passionately held differences of opinion about the "right" way to engineer any machine). In recent years, MP leaders have begun to see the value of employee ideas (thinking) about how best to design and tweak the machine, but this has seldom extended to employee involvement in fundamental business strategies. That thinking is reserved for top managers who can see the big picture. Mechanistic Paradigm leadership is almost always autocratic.

When it comes to the idea of employees making choices, the situation is even worse. The attitude of MP leaders often is that the choice to work here (or not) is the only real choice. They rely heavily on the employment contract, and programs designed to eliminate resistance to "change." Of course, they realize employees are making choices, but these choices have seldom been seen as key to organizational success (except when a strike is immanent). These choices are just one of the inputs to production. As leaders, they must focus on all the inputs, outputs, production process, supply chain management, financial factors, product design, marketplace factors, quarterly earnings, and the trading price of the stock—all of which are appropriate to their role as stewards of the well-being of the organization as a whole. What is missed in all this, however, is that individual human choice is the essence of these "things" called organizations. Organizations are people *choosing* to work together to cooperatively achieve certain purposes.

Much of what has been said about MP leaders could also be said about leaders of the Organic Paradigm persuasion (OP leaders). But their fixation is on the "farm," not the machine. They are concerned with such things as the optimum conditions for growth. Individual human growth is of course given lip service, but the real focus is on the crop. While there is an awareness of consciousness, both thought and emotion, and of choice, attention goes to creating conditions favorable to fruitful thinking and "healthy" choices. Job descriptions, classifications, and policies for fairness dominate. Individuals and teams, finally, are only living creatures responding to their environments. Someone has to take care of them. Organic Paradigm leadership is almost always paternalistic.

Relativistic Paradigm (RP) leaders, on the other hand, are different, or at least they regard themselves as such. They have freed their minds from the shackles of micro-management, whether that be of machines or of farms. Their vision is high. They are focused on the globe, galaxy, and gigabytes. Their concerns are cosmic. The system is the thing. Change is our friend. We must trust the process. It is all delightful and dazzling. And that is the problem. It is so dazzling that something so small as an individual's nagging doubts and fears of loss tend to get minimized. Again, the big picture and its fascination with scientific objectivity blind us to the intensely subjective reality of human consciousness and choice. Relativistic Paradigm leadership is almost always cosmically optimistic.

To compound the problem, understand that all three of these paradigms are operating within today's organizations. They wander through top management strategy meetings, they weave their views through cross-functional improvement teams, they become entangled with problem-solving efforts on the shop floor, clouding understanding, competing for attention, recruiting new partisans to man the barricades of "right." Collaboration becomes confused as one view and then another seems to make sense, but is then discredited by seemingly opposite evidence. Much of this is happening on an unconscious level, in the pre-dawn dimness of assumptions. In spite of sincere best efforts, agreement and alignment are constantly frustrated. These paradigms create far more misunderstanding than the much publicized personality styles.

It's time for a new, more realistic paradigm of organizations. That paradigm is one of conscious systems.

The Paradigm of Conscious Systems

Conscious systems are systems in which consciousness and choice have become determinant. To say that differently, when a system is no longer purely mechanical due to the human element interacting with it, the functioning of that system is ultimately *determined* by human choice, no matter how unaware that choice and no matter how limited the person's consciousness may be.

When we cross the threshold into conscious systems, we must think differently and become aware of a new set of forces, dynamics, and laws—the laws of consciousness. Two things must change in our thinking. First, we must remember that people have the choice to give or withhold their ideas, commitment, and energy. This calls for processes that help them make these choices consciously. Second, we must realize that in such systems, for the first time, the parts (individual human beings) have purpose and meaning independent of the system. Carburetors have no purpose without cars, and hearts have no purpose without human beings, but human beings have purposes independent of the social and ecological systems of which they are a part. And they bring those purposes to work with them. This calls for organizations that value the individual human being as a person, not just for her or his contributions to the company. And it calls for organizations that find a way to integrate those purposes—convergent organizations.

In the Paradigm of Conscious Systems, the universe is seen as matter and energy, but it is also seen as mind-spirit. It is understood to be infinitely changing and eternally expanding. Consciousness is growing itself. It is machine thinking that is winding down; it is mechanical human systems that are breaking down. Conscious systems and the universe are winding up.

Causality, in this paradigm, is seen to sometimes be the interaction of creative consciousness (cosmic scale and human scale) colliding with the continuities of prior creations, creating change. At other times, causality is mechanical chance. Complex phenomena have multiple causes rather than singular or "core" causes. Change at the human level and perhaps at the cosmic level results from either chance or choice, or a combination of the two. It may be slow, mechanical, and evolutionary, but because of the quantum power of consciousness, it can also be rapid and sometimes even instantaneous.

Organizations are understood to be conscious systems. Individuals are recognized as interdependent points of consciousness and choice in these organizational systems. They are the fundamental units of organization. Imagine organizations as complex conscious systems in which various continuities and thousands of individual choices are determining what happens. Teamwork is conceived of as synergistic alliances of aligned individualism. Committed teamwork is the goal, not boundary defense. And finally, leaders are thought of as stewards of the mutual enterprise whose purpose is the well-being of the organization as a whole.

The main beliefs that guide leaders who have internalized the Paradigm of Conscious Systems are the same as previously stated:

1. Individuals are the fundamental units of organization. They are not tools of production. They are conscious beings who exercise personal choice. Each individual counts. In today's world, individualism is indispensable. There are always *legitimate* differences in self-interests, opinions, and beliefs. Differences are valuable. They serve as raw material that fuels the organization's engine. The vision here is of a new birth of individualism that understands its interdependence.

2. Teamwork is the essence of organization. It is not just a desirable behavior. We all need help from others. No individual is completely independent and today all jobs are interconnected. Teamwork at its best is aligned individualism. The vision here is of teamwork free from peer oppression and provincial protectionism.

3. Leadership is the galvanizing vision and energy of organization. It brings people together in service of the common enterprise. The legitimate aim of leadership (authority) is the wellbeing of the whole. The organization as a whole is a conscious system which exists as its constituent parts within an ecology of interdependent exchange. The vision here is of leaders that see the whole of the organization in each employee and in every team as they work together to serve the needs of their customers, communities, and the world. Leadership is the art of understanding the needs and interests of all involved and of finding a convergence of interests that propels the performance of the organization.

ACTIVELY CHANGING YOUR BELIEFS

Perhaps the views presented in this chapter helped you unload some old beliefs. If so, it was because the "proofs" offered by the argument allowed you to claim what you already knew in your soul. Perhaps the views presented here merely frustrated you, and you were wondering why you were reading this and what in the world the practical application of it might be. The application is to your own mind. If you do not change the beliefs in it, you will not be able to provide the kind of leadership that is required in our time. You will play with techniques; you will dally in involvement; you will talk the language of pioneering vision and of convergence; but you will be faking it. And sooner or later, you will fall back into your old beliefs and the leadership practices that go with them. If by now you truly believe you want to catalyze and lead a pioneering organization, your first act of leadership is to pioneer the changes in your own mind.

Leading the Pioneering Action Plan

12

Yes, this book is about pioneering organizations, but it has a secondary purpose: to give leaders an action plan. In so much of the leadership literature, the leaders seem to be standing still. The picture we get is from tombstone testimonies and calcified characteristics. Or we are given smoky brown lithographs of their visions and trophy plaques with their values on them. I have done some of that in this book as well. But that is not enough. The job of leaders is to get people working together with energy and commitment toward the achievement of common goals—a very dynamic, action-packed job when it is done well.

Real leaders are not people pontificating from a glass and glitter tower or handing down orders like some Moses who's staying on the mountaintop. They are not people who spend all of their time in a boardroom or at lunches with bankers. Most of all, they are not people closeted with their computers. They are out there, talking to people, seeing what is going on, connecting, and telling people they are doing a great job. Real leaders have an action plan. Here's one for pioneering.

THE ACTION PLAN

The Checklist presented in Chapter 7 provides the framework for daily, continuous, in-the-thick-of-things leadership. That will go a long way toward developing the full potential of any organization. But if that is the only leadership tool and the only change strategy, it will take a long time to get to pioneering. This chapter provides some jump-start strategies in the form of action plans for developing pioneering organizations. The major concepts of the book are summarized in these action plans.

Here are the steps:

1. Develop a pioneering purpose
2. Lead the convergence and commitment process
3. Rally individualism
4. Establish teamwork in all directions
5. Build a culture of communication and trust
6. Ensure supportive processes

Step 1: Develop a Pioneering Purpose

It is time to take action on the first leadership commitment described in Chapter 6:

I will create an organization that people see as a good place to work. I will dedicate myself to achieving commitment to our vision and earning the trust of our employees.

As was just mentioned, the job of leaders is to get people together working with energy and commitment toward the achievement of common goals. "Come together right now," is a phrase from the Beatles song by the same title; it is also the theme song for a provocative Nortel television commercial, but it is not just a cute idea. It is what it takes. The first order of business is to get people together. It is time to sound reveille.

Curiously, this is not what usually happens. Often, new leaders are getting their programs together instead, meeting mostly with staff and top managers. Certainly it is a good idea to have a program, but by the time leaders get around to talking with workers about it, it is often too late. At least it is too late to catalyze the kind of commitment that powers pioneering organizations.

That begins with leaders going to the people of the organization with a pioneering vision—not one that is polished with the details all worked out, but instead, one that can be stated as a simple, compelling description of the breakthrough the leader hopes to achieve. For example, Ford's vision of wanting to build a "motor car" that everyone could afford. Or Jobs' vision of the revolution personal computers would bring. Or Webber and Garber's vision at Vignette of creating an organization that was a good place to work. The details come later. They are created by the people who are drawn to the vision—the people of the pioneering organization.

To say that the first priority for any leader should be "getting people together" is not a matter of public relations or paternalism, it is a recognition of the essential nature of organizations, their dynamics, and the role of leaders in catalyzing energy for the common venture. It is a matter of affirming that leadership authority is, in part, from and for the benefit of those who work there. It is a matter of leadership legitimacy. "Hired hand" is no longer a viable employee metaphor.

Developing a sense of purpose in an organization begins with an action plan for heightened consciousness. That means getting people together and focused on their common purpose and challenges— waking them up. It is so easy for people to go to sleep on the job, particularly in large organizations. That does not mean people aren't working hard and thinking a lot. In fact, most of the time they go to sleep because they are working too hard and thinking too much about how to get everything scheduled and done. They forget why they are doing it—what they are trying to accomplish for the organization and for themselves. That often results in them feeling burdened and resentful and in a state of constricted consciousness. Organizations are conscious systems. Constricted consciousness is not good for business.

There are a variety of group meeting formats that will get people thinking and working together. It is not a delicate process and does not really require a precise design so long as it provides opportunity for dialogue. The "gathering" outlined at the last of this chapter is an example. Keeping everyone aware and awake and remembering *why* they are together in the first place is the most important thing any leader can do. This should perhaps be the real meaning of the word *organize*—creating the consciousness of being an organization. It is to create a moment in which people look at each other and realize they have a lot on the line together. This consciousness is where the river of organizational performance begins. It is the headwater.

A development strategy for heightened organizational consciousness takes the form of discussions and deliberations focused on what the organization is trying to do and the challenges it faces in doing it. News releases will not serve. Nor will newsletters, CEO videos, flowery vision and mission statements, or any other form of one-way communication. It takes talk. Straight talk, tall talk, stories, debates, and comments on the weather. E-mail can serve to supplement the process, as long as some of the dialogue is live. People need to think about and then talk about their common purpose. This is what creates the sense of belonging, the sense of identification with the organization. When the discussion gets animated, when people get excited talking about the adventure, the pioneering spirit is evoked.

This is the way people get committed to a vision, not by seeing a slick PR piece. They talk about it. They critique it, adapt it, improve it, and ultimately end up giving it their best—particularly when they get to add some wrinkles of their own, things that they have envisioned that might fix some problem a customer is having. People work hard when they are proud of their organizations. Thinking about and talking about what they are trying to do together gets them in touch with the way the organization is helping other human beings. It gets them in touch with their desire to make a contribution, to make a difference in people's lives and in their communities. They are able to *see* and *feel* the importance of their work. They share a vision. It is no longer someone else's vision.

This kind of gathering is the opportunity for people to gain a personal sense of purpose for their contributions to achieving the vision. It can happen as simply as suggesting the basic vision and asking everyone present to reflect on the possibilities. Any ideas they have can be written on note cards and put up for consideration by all. Even a small amount of time spent on this kind of thinking can produce breakthrough ideas.

In efforts to develop a pioneering purpose in their organizations, leaders should set two goals for themselves:

1) to achieve extraordinary levels of *commitment,* and
2) to achieve a *convergence* of the interests of individuals, groups, and the organization as a whole.

When these two conditions exist simultaneously, they create an accelerator for extraordinary levels of aligned action—a prerequisite for any peak performance, particularly the performance of pioneering organizations. Commitment occurs within individuals. Convergence occurs within groups and within the organization. Getting people together can serve both of these goals. Designed correctly, such organizational "gatherings" are a kind of symbolic reenactment of the founding of the organization. They renew a collective understanding of the purposes for being together and confer membership in the community. They recreate the heightened consciousness that exists when people choose to create organizations. The large quarterly meetings for all employees in each Starbucks city are excellent examples.

Developing purpose in their organizations also requires leaders to think and act in terms of the whole. Organizations are living conscious systems, not a collection of functions and divisions held together by plans. Organizations are a state of mind. They are an awareness of interdependence and interconnected action. That awareness grows stronger when members get together to talk about the organization—its goals, challenges, and ways they can help make it better. Awareness is heightened further when members can feel leaders serving the interests of all. That is what creates trust in the leadership. This kind of leadership is the role of chieftains, not warriors, and chieftains are in short supply these days.

Developing organizations that are faster, more flexible, and more responsive—pioneering organizations—is the goal. It is first about developing *organizations*. Putting together opportunistic networks of providers linked only by electronic systems and employing only temporary workers may be a good way to increase profits, but networks are not organizations. They do not have the glue of common purpose required for pioneering.

Step 2: Lead the Convergence and Commitment Process
Second, leaders must bring the following commitment to life:

I will ensure that throughout the organization there is agreement about what we are doing, how we are doing it, and commitment to our plans.

Choice is occuring whether leaders lead it or not. The choice to commit or to hold back is an inalienable human right that cannot be "managed" since it cannot be seen. It is possible to "give" workers choice about what they do or how they do it. It is possible to manage that. But it is not possible to give them choice about how much of themselves they put into doing something. They already have that choice, and they are exercising it on a daily basis in ways that make organizations winners or losers. Leaders cannot control this decision making; they cannot force compliance, but they can learn how to create and lead processes that make use of it as a source for organizational power.

Employees are continuously assessing the organizational situations around them, deciding whether to commit or to hold back. Much of this assessment occurs at a subconscious, instinctive level. The conclusions and consequent choices are often poorly informed. Leaders can enhance and tap this natural process as a means of developing organizational performance. Too often, leaders ignore the process, wrongly believing that compliance will result from clear directions. At other times, they may even attempt to suppress it, leading to employee resistance and resentment. Attempts to "empower" employees with this choice are typically met with inner laughter at the paternalism. Recognition is what is needed. By acknowledging the existence of this natural assessment process and honoring it, leaders are then in a position to lead it.

Leading choice processes involves calling them out into the open and making them a matter of organizational business. This is the real purpose of participation and employee involvement. However, for such processes to work—for them to result in open, truthful discussion—leaders must be willing to reveal their own doubts and concerns, their own assessments and conclusions. In so doing, they become part of the community, not above it. They participate in membership.

Creating processes for open deliberation and decision making also enhances the quality of information available for employees to make informed choices. They make better decisions, and they get clear on what it takes to work together effectively. They are no longer simply following instructions with no idea how their work links with the work of others.

The most important outcome, however, is that planned open sessions raise this instinctive assessment process to a conscious level. People become aware of the choices they are making and what those choices will likely produce. They also become aware of extraordinary possibilities—opportunities they had not thought of before. And they see how their actions can make a difference. Organizations are conscious systems. The greater the consciousness, the greater the organization.

But open community discussions are not enough. When the expectation is for anything less than full commitment at the end of the process of deliberation, such discussions easily deteriorate into gripe sessions, or a lot of talk about what somebody else should do. They produce noise, not action plans. And they certainly don't produce agreement about anything. Pioneering organizational performance requires the development of a commitment culture. Such cultures do not occur naturally. In fact, there are many individual and cultural influences acting against them.

Beyond the instinctive human tendency to self-protect by limiting commitment, people are conditioned by society to be on guard and protect themselves. This is particularly true in organizational life. Over time, this results in a tendency toward caution and guardedness that restricts energy and emotion. This is different from "keeping up your guard" or staying alert while actively defending yourself. This protective tendency is passive. It involves inaction and halfhearted performance. In relationships, a fear of commitment is a common malady in our times. In organizational life, this shows up as a "do what I'm told and no more" attitude. They are both behaviors that hurt others.

Developing a commitment culture requires both individual work and teamwork. For individuals, the work is about increasing personal competence in committing. This is done through meeting processes that develop greater self-knowledge about the internal assessment process, an increased emotional ability to push past fear, and skill in communicating commitment to others.

For teamwork, the development comes from establishing norms for discussing openly and candidly what each is willing and able to do and norms for voicing doubts and concerns. Another important norm is a willingness to stay engaged until all issues are resolved. All of this is developed when leaders involve employees frequently in open deliberations about what needs to be done and, after all issues have been worked through, ask employees to make public individual statements of commitment. As author Will Schutz discovered, people who cannot verbalize a firm "yes" to a plan, even though they have intellectually agreed to it, are not committed to seeing it through.[17]

Step 3: Rally Individualism

Third, leaders must do the following:

I will assure that the organization supports individualism and honors the interests and purposes of every employee.

Individualism is characterized by a lifelong quest for competence and for making a contribution. The human journey toward self-reliant competence is itself a form of pioneering. It requires much of the same spirit. Individualists are also people who want to make their mark. They seek better ways of doing things. They tend to become discontent with the status quo. They believe they can make a difference, and that their ideas can be a contribution in the interests of all. They are also willing to stand up for their ideas and risk the consequences of disapproval. All of these attitudes and behaviors fuel a pioneering spirit.

Commitment occurs in individuals. It is a matter of choice. People who know their own minds and are willing to act on their convictions make the strongest, most dependable commitments. That is individualism. Individualism is not the enemy of extraordinary organizational vision and performance; it is the foundation for them. In our time, individualism is in poor health. Psychotherapy will attest to the degree that people often do not know what they want and lack the confidence to act on it even when they do. Leaders would serve their organizations well by making the development of individualism an organizational priority.

This is not, however, a matter to turn over to the training department, though they can help. The development of individualism requires the consistent and concerted effort of all of the organization's leaders and managers. First, the current team fads that suppress individualism must be stopped. Beyond that, individualism must also be encouraged and developed. Individualism is not something that can be learned in the classroom alone, it must be practiced in the middle of organizational life with all of its consequences. Leaders must call it forth, engage it, and welcome its contributions.

The kinds of collaborative processes advocated in the first two action steps provide an excellent arena for developing individualism. Designing organization meetings and forums so that they begin with individual reflection is the key. Asking people to take a few minutes to think, for example, about current organizational practices and to make notes about the problems they see begins to develop a person's capacity to think independently. Asking them then to share their notes with their colleagues strengthens the capacity for taking a stand. Both of these help them become clearer on their own values and preferences, and this helps them develop their capacity for vision.

Another opportunity comes from using the checklist presented in Chapter 7 as a litmus test in all organization and unit planning activities. When people are encouraged to assess how plans affect them, whether or not their self-interests are served, they develop an increased ability to know their own minds and to know what they want. This brings self-interest to the surface where it can be expressed in healthy ways and aligned with the interests of others, rather than staying submerged in resentful feelings that tend to undermine the best of organizational plans.

Contrary to popular belief, the idea that it is all right to want what we want does not necessarily end in selfishness. When the same respect is extended to others in open forums like these, it actually leads to sharing and generosity. Suppressing these natural desires or making them seem wrong conversely creates a fear of lack and a sense of scarcity that festers into narcissistic self-seeking. Furthermore, an optimistic, can-do, self-reliant attitude can be developed by the radical idea that it is not only all right to want what we want, but it is also possible to get it by working together.

The five strengths of individualism provide the outline for developing individualism in your organization:

- Individualists must feel that they belong, that they count, and that the organization is a place in which they can make a difference and be rewarded for it. The key is in creating opportunities for employees to be involved in making decisions that can help the organization and help them as well. Conditions that cause employees to circulate their resumes outside the company promote me-ism, not individualism.

- Individualists do their own thinking and make up their own minds. Organizational planning must provide them with the opportunity to do that and to offer their views in the open meetings described above.

- In those meetings, people should be applauded for having the courage of their convictions, not shamed or punished for it. Debates should be welcomed. We must stop telling people they are not being good team players.

- Encouraging employees to seek out new opportunities for themselves in the organization—new places where they can make a contribution—helps develop the self-reliance of individualism. HR must get out of this "new road" or find a way to lend a hand, to slightly rephrase Bob Dylan's *The Times They Are A Changing*.

- Finally, individualism is built on the self-esteem that comes from service. Organizations that are focusing primarily on increasing profits for their shareholders will never deserve the honor of individualism's presence. Make sure your organization is living up to its advertised values. Let it begin with you.

Normally, these characteristics of individualism are the traits of only a few. It is your challenge to develop them in women and men throughout the organization. The strategies suggested above will help get it started, but as leaders you must be constantly looking for ways to support individualism when it appears. Recognizing individual contributions is important. Rewarding them will also help. Perhaps most important, however, is clearing the path by getting bureaucratic red tape out of the way. The last action step addresses these red-tape processes.

Individualism is the foundation for healthy teamwork and the fuel for pioneering organizations. Leaders who would take their organizations to the highest levels can only get there by developing a strong tradition of individualism. It is time to rally the return of individualism. While individualism cannot be trained, it can be coached. Leaders who are themselves individualists can help others by instructing them in the behaviors, challenging them in meetings, and cheering them on when they take the field.

Step 4: Establish Teamwork in All Directions

Fourth, leaders must take action on this commitment:

I will help develop teamwork in all directions within the organization, with our customers, our vendors, our communities, and our environment.

Teamwork is a natural human tendency. It is not difficult to achieve. Human beings have been helping each other do things since the origin of the species. It was the principle underlying tribes and villages and nations and organizations. Teamwork is the essence of organization. It is not just a desirable behavior. We all need help from others. No individual is completely independent, and today all jobs are interconnected. Teamwork at its best is aligned individualism. The vision here is of teamwork free from peer oppression and provincial protectionism.

Given everything you have done up to this point, the structure and processes for developing teamwork are already in place. You only need to make use of them. It is essentially quite easy. Mostly all you have to do is show up. It is crucial that you and all the leaders and managers in your organization participate in the meetings and forums created in the action steps above and in the planning activities that make use of *The Organization Convergence & Commitment Checklist*. As a leader and as a participant, it is your job to ensure that discussions always include an exploration of who will do what and who needs what help from whom. Nothing new here. The rest is facilitation of agreements between all parties, horizontally and vertically. Obviously, agreement is difficult at times, but seldom impossible. For the hard ones, you can bring in an OD facilitator.

The processes described so far are primarily for achieving teamwork within the organization, though it can certainly be productive to include customers and vendors in some of these meetings. Teamwork with customers, vendors, communities, and the environment, however, also require some special action plans of their own. IC²'s approach is to bring together business, education, government, and leaders of community organizations to find solutions that create wealth and share prosperity. This is a good example of teamwork across a system. Early in the book, I described the extraordinary efforts at Ritz-Carlton to work with guests. Such "teamwork" requires policies that empower it rather than policies that cause the employee to work against the needs of the customer. At Starbucks, they have created important programs to improve the conditions for workers who grow and harvest the coffee and for the small family vendors, most of them in poor countries. These programs also promote good ecological practice. Starbucks employees are also involved in local community projects and charities.

At the Outback Steakhouse chain, local managers are encouraged to work with their communities and find ways to help. My son Zach, who at the time was an Outback manager, came up with an interesting way to help a local senior-class fund-raiser designed to get money for a bus to the senior prom (so there would be no danger of driving and drinking). Outback cooked dinner for all those working at the fund-raiser, serving steak, baked potatoes, salad, and "Bloomin Onions" for all the hungry volunteers. At the Post Ranch Inn, employees serve on local boards and volunteer for the fire department and the clinic. The Post Ranch Inn also has one of the strongest ecological programs in the world. It was selected as the first "green hotel" and became the model for the development of standards that are now being applied to hotels worldwide.

This magagement commitment is about teamwork in all directions. Two additional principles will help. The first one is what I call the 4 x 4. Most systems in today's organizations require the collaboration of at least four functions to achieve teamwork across the system. For example, the manufacturing systems I worked with at Abbott Labs required the design engineers, the plant engineers, manufacturing, and maintenance—this was the core group. Other functions, such as

QA and purchasing, also had to be consulted, but did not need to participate in the teamwork deliberations since they were not linked directly by the system. Administrative systems typically require the collaboration of the responsible admin unit, the IT developers, the IT support group, and system users (seen as a function, though end users may represent several different functional units). Product development systems typically require five: R&D, marketing, product engineering, equipment engineering, and manufacturing.

In addition to the (typically) four functions, I learned by hard experience that achieving teamwork also required the participation of four levels of authority for each of those functions, except in flatter organizations in which all levels were required. For example, in the Abbott Labs manufacturing example, the participation of the levels of plant/division management, directors, supervisors, and operators/mechanics were all needed to work out the teamwork agreements. We all know of the "good news up, bad news down" phenomenon in organizational structures, but those levels are also used as an excuse by participants in cross-functional improvement projects. People hide behind them. Furthermore, the performance goals for each level are frequently not linked precisely either vertically or horizontally. Consequently, agreements reached at one level may not be supported at others.

Given all of these factors that naturally hinder teamwork—the differing interests, purposes, and needs of each function and each level—it is no wonder that true "trans-system" teamwork is so difficult. The solution I found was to have the four functions and their four levels all in the room at the same time. The principle is what I call the 4 x 4, a process for gaining teamwork traction in any system.

The second principle is what I call the colleague principle. In developing teamwork agreements, within units or across systems, all who are involved need to see and treat each other as colleagues. This means that people from each function and from each level need to collaborate *as equals* in finding teamwork solutions. The recent concept of seeing system users as customers did not work. It created a kind of "the customer is always right" sense of entitlement that one department used against another.[18] The truth is that they all have to be *mutually responsible* for the total system or it will not work well. Manufacturing should not see itself as engineering's customer, and the accounting department should not see itself as IT's customer. Teamwork means taking mutual responsibility for the overall results.

Step 5: Build a Culture of Communication and Trust

Fifth, leaders must carry out the following commitment:

I will build a culture of communication and trust. Let it begin with me.

Trust is a state of readiness for unguarded interaction with someone or something. Distrust puts up barriers designed to provide protection. Trust is required for agreement, commitment, and teamwork. Trust is required for pioneering organizations. Trust is required for open communication, but communication is also the means for building trust. As a leader, it is your job to advocate and model communication behaviors that build trust.

Communication is the means we use to seek cooperation in meeting needs—personal needs and the needs of work interactions. Making our needs known and being clear about what we are willing and not willing to do, what we have the skills to do, and where we lack them—these are the communication behaviors that build trust. Coupled with an intention to find a convergence of needs and interests, to work for win-win solutions, these are all we really need to build trust. These are the ingredients for what I call tangible trust building.

Given the meetings and processes you have put into motion, there is a unique opportunity to deliberately jumpstart the process of building a culture of communication and trust. First, declare that as your intention. Issue a policy, if you use such formal methods in your organization. If not, simply describe the opportunity of using the meetings for this purpose and advocate it. Model the behaviors yourself and call for them in all of the meetings you sponsor or attend. You can have the training department help. With these actions, you can build a trust culture in your organization.

Maintaining it, of course, means that you must follow through on agreements, take other people's interests and concerns seriously, and see to it that this becomes a company norm. Following through with the action plans described above will go a long way in building this trust. Not responding to the needs and concerns that are expressed is the kiss of death. For a much more thorough discussion of building and maintaining trust, see Chapter 9.

Step 6: Ensure Supportive Processes

Sixth, leaders must achieve the following:

I will ensure that every process within the organization supports convergence, individual expression, and teamwork in all of our meetings and interactions.

This book is about the convergence of individualism, teamwork, and leadership and the effect of that convergence on organizations. A convergence of these primary forces results in extraordinary levels of vision and performance. And yet such a convergence is relatively easy to achieve. Leaders have only to remember that their authority legitimately is in service of all. "Hired hand" organizational thinking will not do it. Focusing only on objectives or on technical solutions will not do it. Organizations are conscious systems in which human choice determines the real outcomes.

To create convergence, leaders must simply make it their business to work in the best interest of all. Using processes like the ones described above as a means for making all needs known, discussible, and, for the most part, achievable is all it takes. The Checklist serves as a guide. For example, in the story of the senior partner at Booz·Allen & Hamilton (found in Chapter 8), it only took a small adjustment to a large plan for it to serve his needs as well as the needs of his team and of the organization. His extraordinary performance more than justified that change.

Up to this point, I have been describing what leaders must do to develop pioneering organizations. Now, it is time to talk about a few things they must undo.

First, stop using surveys as a substitute for direct employee involvement in decision making. Polls are not voting. Satisfaction is not commitment. If you must use a survey to convince yourself that it is time to sit down and talk with the people in your organization, you have missed the point of this book. It is always time. Organizations are people. People must talk about what the are trying to accomplish together. That is the only way to stay on target and to stay committed. The job of leaders is to convene this discussion and through it to protect, defend, and serve the interests of all.

Surveys could tell you whether or not you are doing that, but consulting with your own heart or asking people may be more honest. Surveys do not show concern. In fact, they often create distrust; the results are frequently not clearly actionable, leading to either more questions or some kind of general training program that leaves employees saying, "We told them and they did nothing about it." More telling, however, is that surveys usually involve perceptions about the status quo, not opinions about potential courses of action. It is far more powerful to involve people in deciding what needs to be done and securing their commitment to do it.

Second, beware of show-stopper strategies. I encountered an example recently. It concerned an attempt to increase profitability. The accounting folks decided to help top management achieve this objective, so they tightened up on everyone else, questioning purchases, requiring more documentation, and in fact lowering costs by delaying expenditures. The result, of course, was to throw a kink into the supply chain, causing "just too late" deliveries, alienating customers, and slowing revenues. Profitability sagged.

Too frequently, managers focus only on streamlining production systems and ignore the "control systems" that are eating the organization's lunch. The strategies suggested throughout this book increase choice, convergence, and commitment—not attempts to control.

This leads us to the third action needed to clear the path for pioneering to begin. Reengineering needs to begin in the control functions. That is where the "system," as Deming[19] called it, most constrains choice, creates red tape that makes convergence difficult, and frustrates commitment. The control functions—financial, purchasing, inventory, human resources—were all originally designed to serve top management. They are by their original charter "hired hand" systems. These charters need to be undone. Like quality control, these functions need to be put into the line and designed to serve, support, and facilitate those who must get the job done. This will do more to liberate the pioneering spirit than any other single action.

BEGINNING THE PIONEERING JOURNEY
WITH A TOTAL ORGANIZATION PLANNING SYSTEM (TOPS)

At several points, I have advocated involving all employees in the organization's strategic planning processes. Earlier, I referred to a "gathering" designed for this purpose. Here are the essential steps:

1. Hold a "town meeting" discussing the strategic issues facing the organization. Have everyone in the same big room or arena if possible. Use many rooms and electronically connect them if not. It is important for most of the organization's employees to participate at the same time. A representative team of employees and managers (both vertical and horizontal) supplements the management team as a fishbowl deliberative group with structured participation from the floor. Include a period for working the business math *with* the employees; do some of it *live* on a projected white-board, only supplemented by prepared graphs and charts. One of the issues must involve ways that employees can work to preserve their jobs and grow them—a strategic jobs policy. This increases trust and the sense of belonging. And the last issue of the day must be the search for pioneering possibilities.

Even if nothing dramatic comes forth at the time, it catalyzes a pioneering spirit to go out and find better ways to do things, to discover and create new possibilities for the human race.

2. Given suggestions offered in the town meeting, have the management team and the representative team develop strategic initiatives.

3. Hold another town meeting to report the strategic initiatives and to involve everyone in operational planning. After the report and an open-mike discussion of the strategic directions and goals, ask functional units to develop ways to support the plan.

4. Have all units complete operational planning. Facilitators can assist the functional units. No special training is needed. Methods for simple identification of priority actions will suffice. Usually employees know what needs to be done. The Checklist can serve as a guide to checking plans for commitment. Staff units should be deployed to participate in line unit deliberations and vice versa.

5. Use an implementation alignment team to serve as a clearinghouse for all plans. The job is to align and integrate, not approve.

6. Hold quarterly town meetings to discuss progress.

There is nothing fancy here. It is a basic outline for involving the organization in its business. It is everybody's business. The process will, of course, require full disclosure and authentic collaboration. This must include deliberations about what work will be done, where it will be done, and who will do it. Downsizing in the night must stop.

The process outlined here is a simple, straightforward one, but it can be powerful in developing commitment and convergence. It provides a *structure* for developing and leading pioneering organizations. The Epilogue that follows provides the spirit.

Epilogue: A Passion for Pioneering

To this point in history, pioneering has been a path chosen by only a few. Everyone else has been taking care of the practical business of everyday life—tending the home fires, providing for the needs of the day. Both paths are honorable and make a needed contribution. It is, therefore, a radical idea to suggest that most people might be involved in pioneering. In a way, however, they always have been. Vicariously, they have followed the exploits of those who went ahead and celebrated pioneers' struggles and triumphs. Pioneering is native to the human spirit. Something in us all yearns for such adventures. Something in us all wants to open new possibilities for humankind. We are all bathed by the confetti of the hero's parade.

There is an unprecedented opportunity for pioneering. No longer are most people required to care for daily needs. Technology has liberated us to take on new challenges. This radically changes the potential of the human race. Breakthroughs are possible everywhere. Breakthroughs are needed everywhere. This is the time for organizations that will answer the challenge. Those that step forward will be popular places to work. Their visions will tap that part of the human spirit that seeks new ways, that yearns to move beyond.

Today, most of us work in organizations. What we could not do individually, we can do together. We can involve ourselves *directly* in the pioneering mission. This is a calling that goes deeper than our desire to achieve peak performance. It touches something in the soul, something spiritual. But it will not respond to leaders who are only profit seeking and pragmatic. It responds to a vision for breakthroughs. It responds only to leaders with a passion for pioneering.

THE SPIRITUAL CORE OF PIONEERING

Throughout this book, I have presented a great many concepts, principles, models, and practices that can be used to lift organizations to their highest performance potentials. That is a worthy goal. But pioneering is something beyond, something more central to our purpose on this planet. Many people are drawn forward by curiosity; many people defy death to get "there" first; many people seek their fortunes in undeveloped and underdeveloped lands; but we do not call them pioneers. Pioneering is more than adventuring or getting there first or earning a mention in the *Guinness Book of World Records*. Pioneering is risking the unknown in search of something that might benefit us all. It is heroic action in service of a noble purpose.

THE LEGITIMATE BUSINESS OF PIONEERING

To a degree, any form of action intended to create a breakthrough that benefits others could be seen as pioneering. Unprecedented production, solutions for long-standing problems, new inventions, and record profits are all beneficial breakthroughs that have become commonplace in today's lean organizations. But do they have that quality that stirs the spirit? Seldom. Pioneering requires not only extraordinary performance, but extraordinary vision as well—vision that encompasses an organization, its customers, and its community. The pioneering spirit and its extraordinary energy is evoked only by breakthroughs that benefit them all.

Even so, there are countless opportunities for pioneering in every industry, in every profession, and in every marketplace. With the launch into cyberspace, history has shown us once again that those organizations that blaze the trail stake out the best places in the new territory. That is proper. They have earned their reward. But only those that continue to serve can stay there. Pioneering is good for business when business is good for people.

PIONEERING THE COMMON GOOD

The dawn of this century sees the human race poised on the brink of a great choice. We have reached a place when the solutions to centuries-old problems are at hand. The pioneering industrial and information economies have provided an unprecedented portion of the human community with unparalleled prosperity, and it appears possible for the first time to extend that opportunity to all. We have conquered many diseases, extended human life dramatically, and are on the verge of discoveries that can usher in an age of universal health. We are enjoying an extended period of relative peace, and many long-standing conflicts have found the beginnings of resolution. We have achieved a level of cooperation that extends worldwide. While there are exceptions, for the first time it is possible to say that there is a human community, one that is approaching unity—the people of the planet earth. The global television coverage of the dawn of this new millennium was testimony to this worldwide community.

And yet there has been a great cost to get to this point, and there are also great dangers. We have depleted many of our natural resources and polluted our planet. We are in danger of destroying its potential to support human life. The uneducated of the earth are being left behind, forming a breeding ground for new hatreds, violence, and disease. We have lost touch with our youth; they have become exiles and now form a refugee culture in our land. Violence is breaking out at our very doors.

Even with these signs of danger, it is tempting to stop and rest in this newly achieved abundance. It has taken so long to get here. Why not just enjoy the wealth for a time? We face a decision: whether to linger, basking in these springtime breezes, or to resume our journey forward—to set out again on our quest to achieve life, liberty, and prosperity for all. For the first time in human history, the technical means for these great accomplishments are available. What is needed are the extraordinary capabilities of pioneering organizations to take us to these long-dreamed-of goals.

Beyond the missions of our separate organizations, there are pressing problems that face us all. It is time for a new kind of partnering—a partnering of organizations in search of the common good. Private agendas alone will not serve. It is time to take back the public agenda from the selfish, power-hungry few. And also to take it back from the myopic movements and moralistic terrorists. It is time to set an agenda for the human race. There is no laissez-faire god who will solve it all.

Our time calls for pioneering. Let's look at some of the pioneering purposes that could galvanize us all. We cannot hide behind an excuse that the problems of the human race cannot be solved. They need only our mutual commitment and our passion.

Determined efforts to eliminate poverty and disease for all humankind are causes that are still worth the best we have to give, in spite of certain religious and political beliefs advocated by a few—often to protect the privileges of that few. Not only must we preserve life, but we must find new ways to nurture the quality of life. Newer and faster could become self-defeating. The soul requires some familiarity and slow dancing. But before we ticket the speeding enterprises of the information world, we need to value the benefits they are bringing in terms of increased global understanding, mutual respect, and perhaps eventually world peace. These are certainly purposes worthy to be called pioneering. Anything that would truly bring the benefits of education and the joys of learning to all would be a pioneering breakthrough. And we must preserve our planet, or all pioneering will have ultimately been in vain. This is the stuff that stirs the pioneers in our souls.

This need to pioneer the common good calls for convergent leadership. Pioneering organizations must provide that leadership. We must come together to take back the agenda from the radical fringes of both the left and the right. We must rescue it from the clutches of the selfish few and their paid politicians. It is time to stop being proud of having the best government money can buy. It is time to claim that we *are* the people. We are the ones who can do it, the ones who have proven ourselves in pioneering our own organizations. We must form a common purpose. I am issuing the call. I hope you will join me.

APPENDICES:
PIONEERING TALES

$\mathbf{P}$ioneering organizations begin with visions, with dreams of unheard-of breakthroughs that can be of great benefit to others—dreams that are higher than mountains and more magnetic than the frontiers they challenge. Pioneering visions are the most powerful forces on earth other than the magnificent forces of the earth itself.

This section is about the organizations those visions create. Four of them are described here in some detail. The intention is to catch them live, whole, with their torches held high, so you can get a sense of what it is like when the five conditions of pioneering organizations all appear at once in one organization. That is a wonderful occurrence, and one that before this time has been too infrequent.

The four organizations were selected for a variety of reasons. Others could have been included. I chose these because they represent different sectors and different industries. I also wanted to tell about organizations with which I had some firsthand experience. One of these organizations is well-known, the others less so. All of them are examples of all five pioneering principles, some to a greater degree than others in any particular organization. But each of these organizations has worked hard to become the kind of organization that it is. They are worthy of any and all praise. Let the parade begin!

A Vision Called Vignette

By Leah Mathison

On seeing its hallways, the world headquarters of the Vignette Corporation in Austin, Texas, doesn't look like the typical quiet beehive of an American corporation. The brightly painted walls, energetic curves of aluminum, and funky lights hung low in corridors and conference rooms seem to emit electric vibes. Everything is full of energy. But the true source of this vibrancy is, of course, the people who exhibit the Vignette values, so carefully constructed, woven, and mirrored throughout the organization.

What was the impetus for this culture—one so strong it permeates the senses of employees, visitors, partners, and customers? At the new-hire orientation each month, Neil Webber, co-founder and CTO, tells the story.

In the fall of 1995, Neil Webber and Ross Garber, former Vignette CEO, found themselves in a position familiar to many working Americans. They hated their jobs. It wasn't necessarily the work they were doing, but they were uninspired and even less interested in the mundane, corporate dronehood of their existence. However, they had a notion of how it could be better. They spawned the Vignette culture long before a product or service was identified. Their quest to incorporate rested on a commitment to a fun, yet adult environment of open information.

An atypical beginning could only be coupled with an atypical way of selecting their offerings. Webber and Garber, both coming from software backgrounds, knew they wanted to do something related to the Internet, but they did not know what. So they set out to discover what the market needed. "We conducted our own informal research, which was as simple as asking business executives what they needed on-line," says Webber. This search led to the company's first product. Vignette opened its doors providing production management for static HTML Web pages. An uncrowded space at the time, Vignette automated the back-end processes and solved the problems of large Web sites. Essentially, Vignette was a vision now established with a product, a service, and bricks and mortar.

But they didn't leave it at that. As the market changed, so did Vignette, upping the ante by replacing static with dynamic capabilities for companies conducting business over the Internet. The result was StoryServer, software that works in tandem with publishing expertise for start to finish Web publishing and e-commerce solutions.

Today, Vignette is a tangible, thriving business that has grown by leaps and bounds in diversity and numbers since its birth. From a single product and service, through new product development and acquisitions, Vignette is now poised to become the premier full-service e-commerce platform. They already have more customers in their market space than any other company and they are the fastest growing software company ever. "That is because we see our business as customer success," CEO Greg Peters says. "Our growth comes from focusing on that, not on our revenue stream only. We have a unique business model. We do not recognize revenues until our software is installed and our customer is successful in using it. That also gives us the ability to better predict our revenue stream—a fact that is also of value to investors."

Despite the fast and furious growing pains, ask any Vignette employee about the company, and you're likely to hear that the individuals who spend their day within the Vignette architecture love being there.

So what brought this success with employees? One manager has the answer. "Part of the reason people perform at such high levels is that we build internal and external relationships based on trust, honesty, and accountability," asserts Robert Folzenlogen, project manager. One telling example comes early in the company's history. Having just received seed funding, current and new hires were told exactly how much was in the bank and how long it would last. Deadlines were set and achieved because everyone there knew the alternative—by the specified date their paychecks would bounce. Webber explained, "We wanted an open environment where people have access to all the information they needed to make their own decisions and optimally solve problems. It wasn't a fear tactic; it was simply respecting their right, as stakeholders, to know."

Nowadays, after Vignette's highly visible public debut, there are legal constraints that prohibit full disclosure of the company's financials. Beyond that, open information exchange remains commonplace in this organization that is anything but common. Entire company meetings happen quarterly, with plans to increase their frequency; and e-mail, newsgroups, and an anonymous online suggestion box are a few of the ways this company, now made up of more than 1100 employees worldwide, communicates. With that communication comes knowledge, and with that knowledge comes ownership.

Indeed, corporate ownership flows throughout the company, with tangibles such as stock options and bonuses, for all employees, as well as the abstract but powerful understanding of each individual's impact on the business. Decisions are made by those whose work it affects—whether in a smallish, widowless center office or an airy space with a stunning view of the Austin greenbelt. Oh, and by the way, the occupants of the inner offices are the highest level executives in the company. "The people doing the real work of the organization should have the nice offices—they deserve it," remarks Webber. Not exactly the corporate norm.

Jerome Tillotson knew Vignette was special when he interviewed for a technical analyst position. "When I arrived at Vignette, I was led through the purple and yellow hallway, past the pinball and Defender machines, to a room full of beanbag chairs. I had made it through the technical interview over the phone, so basically we sat around in the beanbags and ate lunch while talking about the Internet, Vignette, who had the high score on Defender, and, oh yeah, the job. What impressed me most were the people. I liked them. It was apparent the company invested in all of its people and valued them. Everyone I met was happy, smiled, enjoyed work, took it seriously, and played a mean Defender. This was the environment I wanted to work in. I took the job and haven't yet been disappointed."

A vision, in its truest sense, represents the capacity to see how things can be better. An environment that fosters achievement, risk-taking, inspiration, and camaraderie—this is the vision of Vignette.

The IC² Institute: Their Business Is Convergence

n 1977, a powerful force came into the world. The dean of the Business School at the University of Texas in Austin, Dr. George Kozmetsky, founded the IC² Institute. While connected to the University of Texas, IC² was not part of the Buisness School or any other UT college. For 23 years, IC² has remained a semi-autonomous organization that integrates research, education, and outreach projects focused on technology commercialization and high-tech entrepreneurship. The vision was that IC² would enter on a quest for constructive forms of capitalism that would allow communities and nations to grow and prosper. Dr. Kozmetsky, who had been the cofounder of Teledyne, had exceptional credentials for this mission. He also had an extraordinary network of colleagues in business, government, and academia who could be invited to take part in the quest.

There is nothing so powerful as a pioneering vision, and IC² was just such a vision. As the initial director of IC², Kozmetsky quickly turned its attention to the incredible explosion of technology and innovation that had occurred in the Silicon Valley of California. In many ways, that hotbed of entrepreneurial activity had happened as an accidental convergence of talent, ideas, and a new technology, and it had taken 50 years to develop fully. Kozmetsky formed the purpose of deliberately creating a similar convergence in Texas cities, including Austin. He began by meeting with leaders in business, government, and academia to discuss this idea and the importance of technology commercialization for the state. Oil and cattle were still kings in Texas, however, and initially the idea generated little enthusiasm. Only a few years later, though, these initial discussions began to bear fruit. Others—such as Ross Perot; Bob Inman; Governor Mark White; Henry Cisneros; Pike Powers; Frank McBee, the founder of Tracor; Neal Kocurak, now CEO of St. David's Health Care Systems; and Dean of Engineering and IC² Fellow Dr. Ben Streetman—joined the discussion. The efforts of these leaders were influential in bringing MCC (Microelectronics and Computer Technology Corporation) to Austin. MCC, the first major business consortium in the United States, was founded in 1983 by several large high-tech companies, in partnership with the federal government, to mount a development effort competitive with that of the Japanese.

The leaders who had worked to bring MCC to Austin continued to work with IC² and others to attract technology enterprises to Austin. This resulted in, among other accomplishments, the selection in 1988 of Austin as the site for SEMATECH—the semiconductor industry's new research consortium. This developing convergence of technology and the talent pool provided by the university were major factors in Dell Computer Corporation's (founded in 1984) decision to stay in Austin for its rapidly expanding manufacturing operations and to keep its corporate headquarters there. In 1989, the convergence got another boost when IC² founded the Austin Technology Incubator, one of the first efforts to provide assistance and guidance for start-up technology ventures, and The Capital Network (TCN), now the largest and most successful seed capital network in the United States.

The convergence of all of these forces had an extraordinary result. Literally hundreds of hardware and software companies sprang up in Austin, and other companies moved all or part of their organizations there. In 12 short years, the kind of critical mass that had propelled the Silicon Valley had been assembled in Austin. Between 1990 and 1996, the Austin "city-region" added more jobs in the semiconductor and electronics clusters than did any other region in the world except for Portland, Oregon (a city with a similar industrial convergence and a "consortium" for technical education, The Oregon Graduate Institute).

In recent years, this critical mass has been joined by a wave of IT start-ups, particularly Internet and e-commerce ventures. They have produced some of the most successful IPOs in the country. In turn, this has drawn a number of supporting industries to Austin, such as banks, law firms, accounting firms, and consulting firms specializing in these industries. Austin now ranks in the top five on most lists of the hottest high-tech cities in the United States. It is now a major player with the other hotbed technology cities in the United States and around the globe.

IC^2 borrowed a term, "technopolis," to describe this phenomenon that had been catalyzed in Austin. They are now working with communities around the globe to replicate the Austin success. Their mission is to combine technology, entrepreneurship, and education to improve the world via wealth creation and prosperity sharing. Such a vision and mission may be one of the forces that in this century pioneers the golden age for humanity that I called for in this book.

What exactly then is a "technopolis"? What are its elements? And what expertise, concepts, and practices does IC^2 employ in facilitating the development of them?

First, let's dig into this term *technopolis*. *Techno* comes from the Greek word *technikos*, emphasizing technology, and *polis* is the Greek word for city-state. A recent theory was that, as use of the Internet spread and the cost of transporting goods dropped, people would be able to work wherever they liked and cities would lose their importance. The Internet *has* spread rapidly and transportation costs *are* down, but these vital city-regions or city-states are growing rapidly and have become the most important economic entities on the globe.

IC^2's director, Dr. Robert Ronstadt, has strategically restructured the Institute to be the world's first technopolis-facilitating organization.

IC²'s Technopolis Building Program is now contracting with a dozen city-regions around the world (including several in the United States), and the goal is to be working with 40 to 50 such cities ("emerging techno-regions") within the next 15 years. "This gives us the opportunity to use the knowledge we've gained worldwide," says Dr. Norman Kaderlan, IC²'s associate director for the Technopolis Building Program. "It can mean a quantum gain in accomplishing IC²'s mission." Technopolis building is the primary mechanism IC² now uses for creating wealth around the globe, and it also serves as a mechanism for achieving a more equal distribution of wealth as a means of "sharing prosperity." That is because a technopolis does not just generate jobs, it generates higher-paying, technology jobs, which in turn stimulates other local businesses, thereby again generating more wealth.

IC² sees itself as a combination "think and do" tank. It puts its expertise, concepts, and practices to work to test them in the world— a form of action research—and then it puts the tested ideas to work to benefit humankind. Here is a list of some of its tested expertise:

- *Technology transfer and commercialization*—IC² has worked with both NASA and NOAA (National Oceanic & Atmospheric Administration), as well as many other research entities, to move research findings into commercial application.
- *Entrepreneurship*—IC² recognized three decades ago the central role of the entrepreneur in wealth creation. It has championed and supported the development of entrepreneurial ventures and developed entrepreneurial education used in a number of large corporations and in countries around the world.
- *Innovation*—IC² cosponsors the annual International Conference on Technology Policy and Innovation, which fosters new knowledge for policy making and the commercialization of new technology.
- *Incubating technology ventures*—IC² founded the Austin Technology Incubator that has provided support for nearly 100 start-up ventures. Cumulatively, these ventures have realized

nearly $1 billion in sales revenues. Five have gone public. Several others are preparing public offerings or have been acquired at a substantial gain. Less than 9 percent have failed since 1989.

- *Prosperity sharing*—IC²'s primary strategy for prosperity sharing is the development of technology enterprises that generate higher-paying, technology jobs. Beyond that, IC², through its Entertech project, has partnered in the development of educational programs to bring unemployed and underemployed people into the entry-level, high-tech jobs.

- *Transparent technology*—One of the IC² Fellows at the UT Health Science Center in San Antonio, Dr. Antonio Furino, has pioneered the development of strategic management software (SMART) for community-based health organizations. Dr. Furino, who has specialized in technology transfer, says that it is "no *Field of Dreams*. You cannot just build it and they will come." As a result, SMART was designed to allow community health care staff members to do their work using software that "automatically" prepares all of their needed reports, performs other strategic and operational management tasks, and even prepares funding requests. "The key to the future," Dr. Furino says, "is to develop technology that is transparent enough, practical enough, and sufficiently inexpensive that ordinary people will be able to use it intuitively without getting a degree in it or enrolling in extensive training." SMART is now entering a Beta phase with other community organizations, and in the near future it is hoped that it will be available to small- and middle-sized businesses.

- *Innovative education*—IC² offers a Masters of Science in Science Technology Commercialization (MSSTC), a one-year program featuring a global classroom learning environment. Live classes are held between students in Austin, Mexico, Australia, and Portugal. Executive students (28 to 55 years old) assess real technologies, work in global teams, and write business plans for the most promising technologies. Dr.

Barbara Fossum, MSSTC's director, not only has solid academic credentials, but she has worked in major corporations and founded her own successful ventures. She is therefore well prepared to ensure that this program is not just academically sound, but that it is a hands-on, entrepreneurial experience that seamlessly enters into the business life of its students, graduates, and sponsoring countries.

- *Non-traditional education*—IC^2 offers a variety of other executive education programs supportive of the IC^2 vision and mission for businesses and governments all over the world.
- *Expertise dissemination*—IC^2 makes its findings and expertise available through the publication of books and articles as pioneers in multimedia dissemination. It also initiated or supports numerous networks that extend the reach of IC^2's valuable technology commercialization information.
- *Global programs*—IC^2 conducts, sponsors, or supports a number of global programs, including the Japan Industry and Management of Technology Program (JIMT), the International Management of Technology and Training Program (MTTP), the Globally Networked Entrepreneurship Program, and the Corporate International Student Internship Program. Its director, Dr. David Gibson, speaks of "bands of convergence—links around the world, based on common interests, pulling people together."

The IC^2 Institute is in the business of convergence. From its early pioneering vision, to its spectacular success in Austin, to its increasing global impact, IC^2 is committed to—even passionate about—making the world a better place. Its founder and early leader, Dr. George Kozmetsky, had a profound gift for bringing people together, a characteristic that in this book I have suggested is the essence of leadership.

David Gibson fondly tells of one example of Kozmetsky's style of leadership. At a morning mixer just before the opening of an international conference, a woman was enthusiastically engaged in an animated discussion and, without thought, asked the little guy walking by (she thought he was a waiter) to bring her a cup of coffee and a donut. Without hesitation, George Kozmetsky got her the coffee and donut and then proceeded to the podium to open the conference.

The current director, Bob Ronstadt, is seen by the IC² staff as a leader in the Kozmetsky mold, who creates a convergence of interests in everything he does and who is inspiring them to build a strong organization that can truly make a difference in the world. "I'm proud of my colleagues at IC²," he says. "Our challenge is to take IC² to the next level. That means teaching decision makers about the importance of contracting for the long-term help of a technopolis-facilitating organization like IC² to accelerate the development of their high-tech regions. It means expanding our programs, our partnerships, and our IC² Fellows (from 170 to 1,000) over the next decade. It means creating a virtual network, unlike anything the world has seen, devoted to wealth creation in environments of constructive capitalism—a network that reduces the gap between the 'haves' and the 'have-nots.'"

The
Post Ranch Inn:
A Tradition
in Pioneering

3

Driving down the coast highway of the Big Sur in the open-top convertible with the sea breezes whipping around us, filling our senses with mixed scents of seaweed, salt, redwood, cedar, and wild sage, and the to-make-you-cry views of mountains and ocean and crashing waves and the amazing colors and indescribable light that bathes that coast, we were quite justifiably in high spirits. But we were also anticipating our first stay at the much-heralded Post Ranch Inn. So many things in life disappoint. The Post Ranch Inn did not! From the moment we entered that sanctuary, to the "Have a glass of wine" first greeting at guest registration, to the bell man's enthusiastic description of activities available to us at the Inn, to the way that our luggage, camera, and personal items simply appeared in the room ready for use when we were able to tear our attention away from the beauty of the view and the tasteful, simple elegance of the cottage, our spirits rose higher and higher. It began as a spiritual experience. And it continued that way. It was like being granted entry into the joys of God's purest creation. We found ourselves whispering in the reverent, vibrant stillness surrounding us. That was in 1994. I have been a guest three times since. The Inn and its ambience have only grown more inviting each time.

The Post Ranch Inn is a unique resort, opened in April 1992 on Highway 1 about 30 miles south of Monterey, California. It consists of 30 guest suites nestled among a redwood grove on the edge of a mountaintop, 1,000 feet above the Pacific. It also features the Sierra Mar, a five-star restaurant, one of the most spectacular views on the coastline, and a 106-degree, zero-edge pool that seems to float over the ocean.

The Post Ranch Inn grew out of the vision of Billy Post, his wife Luci, and Mike Freed, a local attorney, and his wife, Janet Gay Freed, an interior designer. They wanted to create a special environment in which guests could restore their spirits while wrapped in the inspirational beauty of the Big Sur coastline. Larry Callahan, who joined them as the general manager, enriched this vision. Larry had been the project director for the Nature Conservancy managing Santa Cruz Island and a project manager for development in Jacques Cousteau's U.S. operations. "We didn't know exactly what we wanted the Inn to be," said Larry, "but we knew that we did not want it to seem like yet another hotel. We wanted people to have an intimate experience with nature and to regain some of their wonder and awe for its beauties. But it needed to be comfortable if it was going to attract a professional clientele. We imagined it to be something like 'adult camping'."

Some of the suites at the Post Ranch Inn are separate cottages, others are upper/lower duplexes, and others are small clusters in unique structures known as "butterfly houses" and "tree houses." Each guest room features a private view of the ocean or mountains, a king-sized bed, a private deck, an indoor slate spa tub, a fireplace, and a minibar filled with exotic complementary snacks and beverages. Everything about each room looks like it was carefully selected and placed there for your pleasure. The Inn also offers daily, guided nature walks, stargazing, a lap pool, and a yoga yurt.

The experience of early guests at the Inn was so positive that word-of-mouth rather than advertising quickly made this the place to go on the Pacific Coast. Early in its second year, the Inn was profitable, and before long, it had attained a 90 percent occupancy rate year round. This success inspired a copycat wave of "boutique resorts" around the world. For the Post Ranch Inn, the success led its partners to create two sister resorts, the Jean-Michel Cousteau Fiji Islands Resort and the Lodge at Skylonda in the coastal range 30 miles south of San Francisco. While these new resorts build on the experience of the Post Ranch Inn, they are not copies. They are uniquely designed to fit their natural settings and to open the wonders of those settings to their guests.

The Post Ranch Inn was born from a tradition of pioneering. In 1848, William Brainard Post arrived on the Big Sur from Connecticut and never left. In 1850, he married Anselma Onesimo, a Costanoan Indian from the Carmel Valley, and they began a family. W. B. Post worked in many different jobs in the Monterey Bay area, but spent much of his free time exploring the still-wild Big Sur coast, hunting grizzlies and deer and trading in buckskin. He founded the first grain warehouse in Moss Landing and opened the first butcher shop in Castroville. In 1860, he and his wife were among the first homesteaders on the Big Sur, and in 1867 they began to build the Post Ranch.

As an early pioneer of the area, Post and his sons cleared trails, built roads (including the first coastal road), and established the first postal service in the area. The Post children also married and homesteaded in the area, and his son Joe and his wife, Elizabeth, expanded the ranch to 1500 acres. In 1945, their son Bill and his wife, Irene, opened a small resort and restaurant named the Rancho Sierra Mar. Bill and Irene's daughter, Mary Post Fleenor, ran the restaurant until it was sold in 1972. In 1984, her son Billy and his wife, Luci, in an effort to protect the ranch from being broken up by inheritance taxes, and to share its magnificent beauty with others, formed a partnership with Mike Freed to establish the Post Ranch Inn. And in 1992, as construction neared completion, Larry Callahan joined them.

This pioneering paradise is also a good example of convergence—a convergence of self-interest and service, as well as a convergence of the interests of guests, local artisans, employees, the surrounding community, and owners. While it is every bit a luxury resort, it is also a model for the preservation of the planet earth. The Inn was built in a way that "it required only the removal of one small tree," Billy Post brags, "and we would have saved that one too, but the county made us remove it because it was too close to the road that runs by the cottages." The Inn also worked with the State of California and the Monterey Health Department to pioneer a gray water reclamation plant, used to water the fruit trees and wine grapes. The Inn also composts much of its waste, has been busily bringing back the native grasses, placed and painted its buildings to blend into the scenery, organically grows its own herbs and flowers, and welcomes the wildlife in the area. Larry Callahan proudly points out that the five nearly extinct California Condors that were reintroduced recently in that part of the Big Sur are fond of perching on top of the Sierra Mar restaurant. "Who can blame them," he says.

The Inn has even been kind to the ground squirrels that were digging into the earth-covered roofs of their most expensive units—the separate cottages called "ocean houses." Rather than exterminating the ground squirrels, the Inn undertook the costly effort of reengineering its roofs by putting a waterproof, protective layer between the soil and the ceiling materials—they used one that the ground squirrels did not like to chew on.

Given all their ecological efforts, the Post Ranch Inn was the first "green hotel" and served as a model for the creation of standards that are used in rating other hotels worldwide. This care and reverence for the environment has an additional purpose as well. It sets an example for the guests, many of them in positions of power and influence. It is hard to stay there a few days without becoming an advocate for preserving our beautiful planet.

The Post Ranch Inn continues the Post family tradition of participation in and service to the community. The management of the Inn and its staff serve on local boards and provide help in the operation of the health clinic and the fire department, as well as working with other citizens to see to it that the area has the best possible roads.

This same concern is shown to the 180-person staff. Larry Callahan visits daily with each group to get their ideas and find out what help they need to do the job. But the concern does not stop with job-related problems; Larry and the other managers also see to it that employees get the help they need when there is sickness in their families or other personal problems. The Inn also assists in providing child care for employees and a variety of summer camps for their children. This is in addition to providing the best salaries and benefits in the area, and bonuses based on profitability. "They are not just employees," Callahan says, "they are human beings, and we treat them like we would like to be treated." One of the results is that in the eight years of its existence, the Inn has experienced almost no turnover in staff. "This gives us a unique challenge," Callahan observed. "It makes it harder to get fresh ideas and perspectives. We have to work hard at this. We also work hard on teamwork. One example is that we provide Spanish-to-English and English-to-Spanish classes for all employees. Everybody has to help everybody else communicate."

The Post Ranch Inn's commitment to maintaining excellence in staff and in service is perhaps best exemplified by its policy of inviting all staff and their significant others to be guests at the Inn once a year. As I was checking in on one of my visits, I met one of these employee-guests, a young housemaid and her husband, checking out. "Be sure to try the new Salmon entrée," she said enthusiastically. "They really do something special with it, some fresh herbs from the garden. And don't miss the stars—they'll take your breath away."

So my advice to you is when you need rest and healing after your own pioneering exploits, take a tip from these employee-guests and make your way to the Big Sur and give yourself over to the magnificence of nature's best and the extraordinary care and attention provided by the staff of the Post Ranch Inn.

Starbucks: Pioneering New Cultures

Much has been written in recent years about organizational cultures—creating them, changing them, developing them, and leading them. A great deal has also been written about doing business in the new global economy with its web of social cultural styles and traditions. Cultural diversity in our workplaces has been the subject of thousands more articles and books. What more could be said about culture, you may wonder? Howard Shultz, Starbucks' chairman and CEO, has given us more. Not only did he create a phenomenon that embodies the best practices in all of these cultural arenas, but he blazed new cultural trails as well. Starbucks' success required the creation of an entirely new cultural tradition in the United States, and it also required the creation of a new kind of organizational culture to serve it.

Before Starbucks, coffee drinking in the United States was a popular ritual, but one relegated to a quick cup at home while getting dressed, a cup frequently spilled on the way to work, or the dreadful, dishwater, dark stuff of office coffee pots, rural greasy-spoons, or those misnamed breakfast-grill/lunch-special joints called "coffee shops." The idea of opening a retail store devoted primarily to coffee drinking was absurd, and charging premium prices was even more nuts. Yet today, Starbucks is the most frequented retail store in

America—over 10 million customers a week—and the average customer comes in 18 times a month. This has resulted in a staggering $1.7 billion in 1999 revenues, based on an average sale of only $3.60. "Dropping by Starbucks" is a new cultural tradition perhaps surpassed only by "checking my e-mail."

The cultural pioneering did not stop there. Something very special had to be created to generate and sustain such a demand. It had to be something more rewarding than hula-hoops, pet rocks, or even disco music. It had to be a special place, providing customers with a pick-me-up experience in the midst of their frenetic, stressful lives. Starbucks had to become, as Shultz put it in a recent interview with *Executive Excellence* magazine, a "third place between home and work where people can come to get their own personal time-out, their respite, or to chat with friends." He sees this as a kind of extension of the front porches of an earlier era.

But to achieve the experience of such a special place, the staff and organization serving it had to be something new as well. The workforce drawn to such jobs would essentially be the same as the one drawn to fast-food chains or to low-end restaurants where tipping is sparse—flexible-schedule part-timers, many of them quite young. But how could you get such a workforce to provide the kind of attentive, friendly service that such a place would require? A new kind of organization with a new kind of culture would be required. It had to replace cynicism and resentment with a passion for service and pride in the organization. Starbucks met the challenge.

To achieve such a miraculous change in the part-time workforce, Starbucks pioneered in the creation of compensation, benefits, and working conditions unheard of for such jobs before. They were the first to provide comprehensive health care and stock options for part-time workers; they have added a variety of other work/life benefits and programs supporting employees in such matters as child care, elderly care, and shared interests; they encourage and reward employee ideas and cultivate a democratic exchange between all employees ("partners") and managers. In an industry where annual turnover averages 300 percent, Starbucks has been able to keep their turnover at a relatively low 60 percent. But more telling is the consistent, friendly, good service provided by the staff, and the fact that Starbucks ex-employees—their "graduates"—continue to be some of the best salespeople for the company. "Starbucks is a great place to work," one of them told me. "Starbucks is the way work ought to be."

The Starbucks story is a demonstration of the pioneering principles in a business that most would find uninspiring. Start with a vision of creating new and better possibilities for people; build solidly by creating a convergence of interests for customers, employees, managers, and the community; value the individual human being and encourage individualism; develop teamwork throughout the organization and between employees and managers; and provide consistent leadership in the interests of all, and you will reap the benefits of the power of pioneering organizations. Howard Shultz has done just that at Starbucks.

In their recent book, *Lessons from the Top*, Thomas Neff and James Citrin featured Howard Shultz as one of America's best business leaders. Their choice was based on a Gallup survey of corporate and non-profit leaders, a financial analysis of corporate performance over a five-year period, and the extensive experience of their firm, Spenser Stuart, the world's leading executive search firm. "The spirit of commitment at Starbucks has made it one of the top-performing companies in America. ... Over a five-year period (Starbucks') financial performance was at the top of the Fortune 1000, both on shareholder returns and cash-flow growth." It was for that reason, as well as for the power of the brand that Shultz has developed in a short time, and for his leadership in inspiring his employees to achieve greatness that they chose him. "It wasn't just because he's a terrific guy," Neff said.

In addition to providing an excellent product for its customers, a good place to work for employees, and outstanding financial performance for investors, Starbucks is also very involved in the global community. The company supports a wide range of philanthropic efforts in the communities where it conducts business. It also works for improved business conditions for the small family farmers who grow the coffee beans (most of them in poor countries); works to improve the working conditions and labor standards for agricultural workers who grow, harvest, and process coffee; works to eliminate child-labor abuses in countries where it does business; has played a big role in promoting literacy and providing books; and has partnered with Earvin Magic Johnson's Johnson Development Corporation to develop Starbucks Coffee locations in under-served, inner-city neighborhoods throughout the United States.

In addition, the company has been involved in protecting the environment in efforts such as developing a new environmentally friendly disposable cup, recycling waste, sponsoring and working on green-team local clean-up efforts, using environmental criteria in selecting their store sites, and building "green" buildings. It has even undertaken pioneering efforts in Mexico, South and Central America, and Africa to promote organic and environmentally beneficial growing methods. Given all of these acts of citizenship, I want to say to the self-righteous mob that recently busted up a Starbucks store in Seattle as a side agenda to demonstrations against the World Trade Organization, "SHAME ON YOU."

The Starbucks story is one of creating cultures that lift the human experience. Its values are lessons learned from Howard Shultz's own experiences growing up in a rough, blue-collar neighborhood in Brooklyn. Its people-first policies have given us all a more beautiful "coffee break" to lighten our loads and lift our spirits. It is making a contribution to the world. And it promises to continue to provide a convergence in the interests of us all.

Perhaps the best proof of this is a small miracle that few have noticed. On frequent occasions, Starbuck stores and customers are entirely in the care of very young people with no "adult supervision." Not only are they not sullen and resentful, as is far too often the case elsewhere, but instead these people are providing the same enthusiastic, friendly, fast service we have come to expect when we "drop by Starbucks," and they are doing so with one of the highest levels of teamwork I have ever witnessed. This cultural phenomenon does not exist to such a degree with the youth of

America anywhere else in our society, including churches. This is cultural pioneering that we need to study. Its principles could be the solution to much of the concern and grief we experience with America's youth today.

Notes

[1]Daniel J. Boorstin, *The Americans: The Democratic Experience* (New York: Vintage Books, 1974), p. 548.

[2]Teilhard de Chardin, *The Phenomenon of Man* (New York: Harper & Row Publishers, Inc., 1959), p. 1.

[3]Ron Zemke, *The Service Edge: 101 Companies that Profit from Customer Care* (New York: NAL Books, 1989), p. 477.

[4]Fredrick Reicheld, *The Loyalty Effect* (Cambridge, Mass.: Harvard Business School Press, 1996), p. 10.

[5]These conditions are similar to the conditions Thomas Kuhn postulates for the cause of paradigm shifts in his theory of scientific revolutions [*Structure of Scientific Revolutions* (Chicago: University of Chicago Press, 1962, 1970)]. Walter Prescott Webb, in his book *The Great Frontier* [(Austin: University of Texas Press, 1979), pp. 1-28], saw the two conditions in terms of the necessity created by the crowding and conflict in Europe and the opportunity resulting from the wealth of resources in the New World.

[6]Greed is not new to the human race. The desire to prosper and profit are not in themselves greed. In fact, these motivations can lead to benefits for all. The desire to gain excessively, unequal to contribution, is the real meaning of greed. Gain without contribution is not individualism, it is theft. This type of gain is not acceptable for able-bodied people on welfare roles when jobs are available, nor is it acceptable for corporate raiders and junk-bond sellers whose money adds little value to the companies and often reduces the number of jobs. Some of this is gambling, not investment. And the "house" is losing.

In a discussion I had with the late Congressman Sony Bono on a cross-country flight just before he took office for his first term, we discussed the concept that reward without contribution was theft. From his point of view, supporting such behavior undermines and demoralizes a society and misleads its youth. He invited me to Washington to discuss it further. Unfortunately, we both failed to follow through. I got busy and forgot about it until the news of his death. And perhaps he got sidetracked by the team player pressures of Washington. I'll never know for sure.

Still, I think Sonny valued convergent leadership, and I know he understood individualism from personal experience. I am saddened by his loss. This footnote is my tribute to him.

[7]Larry N. Davis and Diane B. Davis, *Straight Talk* (Austin: Andragogy Press-University Associates, 1982), pp. 36-37.

[8]It would also help to give all employees stock and to make larger percentages available to employees. That way they could also benefit from the rewards of sacrifice. Some of the companies mentioned in this book are doing this.

[9]Dan Cohen, *Business Week*, Oct. 4, 1999, p. 108.

[10]Larry N. Davis and Duane Tway, "Trust and Communication," paper delivered at the 1993 Texas Conference on Organizations, published 1994.

[11]Larry N. Davis and Diane B. Davis, *Straight Talk* (Austin: Andragogy Press-University Associates, 1982), pp. 22-23.

[12]Larry N. Davis and Duane Tway, "Trust and Communication," paper delivered at the 1993 Texas Conference on Organizations, published 1994.

[13]Douglas McGregor, *The Human Side of Enterprise* (New York: McGraw-Hill Book Company, 1960).

[14]Tom J. Peters and Robert H. Waterman, *In Search of Excellence* (New York: Harper & Row, Publishers, 1982), pp. 119-56.

[15]These three paradigms are referred to by various names. The mechanistic is sometimes called mechanical; the organic is called organismic; and the relativistic is called systems.

[16]Peter Block, *Stewardship* (San Francisco: Berrett-Koehler Publishers, 1993), p. 12.

[17]Will Schutz, *The Human Element* (San Francisco: Jossey-Bass Publishers, 1994), p. 205.

[18]One of the leading authorities on customer service, Chip Bell, did not fall into this trap. Rather than advocating a one-up, one-down relationship in either direction, he advocated a partnership. See Chip R. Bell, *Customers As Partners* (San Francisco: Berrett-Koehler Publishers, 1994).

[19]W. E. Deming, *Out of the Crises* (Cambridge, Mass.: MIT Center for Advanced Engineering Studies, 1986). Deming, the creator of Total Quality Management, frequently referred to "the system" in his writing and speaking.

For other resources, visit www.pioneeringorgs.com
Come to the web site to experience:

- Video interviews with industry pioneers such as: Classic Communications, Vignette, IC^2, and many more
- Access to articles by top authors and industry leaders from *Executive Excellence* magazine discussing pioneering themes
- Navigate the path of the Pioneering America Tour and view stories from the frontier
- Discuss the breakthrough work of your organization in our Pioneering Reports (PR) section
- Diagnostics and consultation for the Six Critical Issues of Commitment and how to solve them in your organization
- Access to the Pioneering America Network (PAN) and the Institute for Pioneering the 21st Century
- Information about consulting services
- Sign up to receive a free e-mail newsletter for more stories of pioneering

Index

About the Author

Larry Nolan Davis is CEO of Pioneering, an organizational development consulting firm. For more than 25 years, he has worked with a wide range of organizations, including several Fortune 500 companies. Major clients include Classic Communications, Boeing, Booz·Allen & Hamilton, Texas Instruments, Lockheed, Motorola, and IBM. He has also worked with numerous non-profit organizations, small businesses, and federal, state, and local governments. He is the author or co-author of six books and published off-shelf programs, including *Winning Ways: A Management Simulation*, *Straight Talk: Improving Communications in Your Organization*, and *Planning, Conducting, Evaluating Workshops*, as well as numerous articles in professional magazines and academic journals.

Davis received both bachelor's and master's degrees from the University of Texas at Austin in liberal arts and organization development/human resource development, respectively. His corporate experience includes positions as director of management development, human resource development, and organization development. He has given numerous presentations at national conferences on topics such as training basics, teamwork development, communication, employee involvement strategies, and learning theory. Contact him at

PMB #108
3300 Bee Cave Road Ste. 650
Austin, TX 78746
larry@pioneeringorgs.com
www.pioneeringorgs.com

About the Cover Art

I asked my friend, Warren Cullar, a well-known artist in Austin, Texas, to paint something for the cover of my book. I told him I wanted something with vivid colors to convey the themes of the book—pioneering, individualism, and convergence. He painted an abstract that I loved and that my graphic artist turned into a quick cover.

Initially, the staff at Executive Excellence Publishing also liked it. However, as the weeks went by, they began to focus on an amorphous black shape in the center of the painting that looked like a cat to them. My eyes had also been drawn to this shape. What I saw, however, was the emergence of individualism, silhouetted against a rising sun. I called it "The Sunrise of Individualism." That did nothing for the staff at EEP. They still saw a cat.

In the end, a compromise was reached. One of the graphic artists at EEP digitally distorted the colors of the painting; the "cat" and the "individualist" both disappeared, and type was then superimposed. The cover design you see is the result.

When I showed Warren the final cover, he said, "Well, it is not much like my painting, but I like the colors and the way they set up the print. And it does capture the motion of convergence."

Warren Cullar has rich views about life and his role in it. His views are represented in his paintings. He says that he believes he was born into this life to paint the passions of color. "I am intrigued by colors," he says. "They are the vibrations of the dance of life."

Warren is one of Austin's most prolific and widely collected artists, having placed over 15,000 pieces in collectors' homes and offices during his 30-year career. His most recent artistic theme captures the people, motion, and music of 6th Street in Austin.

Many of Warren's paintings are available for viewing on his Web site.

WARREN CULLAR

12102 Conrad Road   (512) 250-8868
Austin, Texas 78727   warrencullar.com   270

Executive Excellence
publications are perfect:

- *As personal or professional vitamin pills.* Executive Excellence is an enriching monthly supplement to an executive's current diet of management and leadership training. *Personal Excellence* enhances the on-going personal and professional development programs of people at any age and stage in life.

- *As in-house management or personal development newsletters.* The magazines can be customized and received under an organization's own cover sheet.

- *As thought pieces for focus groups and management meetings.* The magazines can be analyzed and applied to help with current organizational dilemmas.

- *As a public relations gesture.* The magazines can be sent to favored suppliers and customers or displayed in reception and reading areas.

- *As gifts.* Executive Excellence may be given to newly promoted managers or to a management segment of the company. *Personal Excellence* may be given to all employees as a benefit.

Custom Corporate Editions
Corporate editions of both magazines are available. The magazine may be wrapped with a "false cover" with messages and announcements from the company, printed with the company logo, enhanced with articles by prominent company officers, or a combination.

Custom Reprints
Order custom reprints of your favorite articles (or chapters in this book)—in black & white or color—for use in your corporate training and development programs and seminars.

Foreign Language Editions
Executive Excellence is available in Spanish, Korean, Japanese, and Turkish editions. English-language editions for Australia, Ireland, and India are also available. *Personal Excellence* is available in Japanese and Turkish languages.

Executive Excellence Publishing has other publications in a variety of languages. For more information on other special editions, please call 1-800-304-9782.